ACTIVITIES FOR BUILDING CONVERSATION

BASICS IN SPEAKING

LINGUAL HOUSE

Michael Rost

Published by
Longman Asia ELT
18th Floor, Cornwall House
Taikoo Place
979 King's Road
Quarry Bay
Hong Kong
fax: (852) 2856 9578
e-mail: aelt@awl.com.hk

and Associated Companies throughout the world

This book was developed for Longman Asia ELT by Lateral Communications Ltd.
Lingual House is an imprint of Longman Asia ELT.

Produced by Longman Asia Limited, Hong Kong
NPCC/01

Development editors: Anne McGannon, Lewis Lansford, Linda O'Roke
Project editor: Linda O'Roke
Project coordinator: Keiko Kimura
Project consultant: Melody Noll
Production coordinator: Eric Yau
Text design: Keiko Kimura
Cover design: Keiko Kimura, Lori Margulies
Illustrations: Kari Lehr, Bruce Day, Mark Ziemann
Recording supervisor: David Joslyn
Photograph coordination: Photodisc, Ken Kitamura, Rubberball, Diamar portfolios

ISBN Textbook 962 00 1425 1
ISBN Teacher's Manual 962 00 1426 X
ISBN Cassette 962 00 1427 8

ABOUT THE AUTHOR

Michael Rost has been active in teaching English, teacher training, and Applied Linguistics research for over 20 years. He has enjoyed teaching in a variety of contexts, including West African high schools, Southeast Asian refugee camps, Japanese intensive language centers, and American teacher training programs. In addition to teaching and teacher training, Michael Rost has been in demand as an educational consultant and as a lecturer. He has worked with the Save the Children Foundation, the Corporation for Public Broadcasting, and DynEd International, and has lectured in numerous countries, including Japan, Korea, Taiwan, Thailand, England, and Denmark. From this range of experiences, he has learned to be sensitive to different students and their purposes for learning languages. Michael Rost is known to teachers internationally as an author of language textbooks (particularly, the *Real Time English* series, *Basics in Listening, Strategies in Listening*), as a development editor (*Impact* Series, *English Firsthand* series), and as an author of Applied Linguistics and teacher training books (*Listening in Language Learning, Listening in Action, Introducing Listening*). Michael has a B.A. in Education (Michigan), M.A. in TESOL (Arizona), and a Ph.D. in Linguistics (Lancaster). He currently lives in San Francisco and teaches at the University of California, Berkeley. You can contact him via e-mail at <mrost@well.com>.

ACKNOWLEDGEMENTS

The author and editors wish to thank the teachers and students who contributed to this project through interviews, reviews, and piloting reports.

In particular, we wish to thank:

Fu-Hsiang Wang	Damon Chapman	Rachel Wilson
Cheng-Yuan Liu	Cate Crosby	Yu-Shiu Chen
Kari Kugler	Steve Coyle	Karen Sutherland
Francois Lambert	Stefan Ptak	James Ball
Ben Dilworth	Kevin Trainor	Kate Murphy
Tim Hawthorne	Gareth Magowan	Simon Balint
Roger Swee	Mei-Yu Chang	

Special thanks go to Grant Trew, Akiko Shinagawa, James Boyd, Stephen Ryan, Craig Smith, Won-Key Lee, and Patrick Wallace, who gave ongoing advice on the project.

We would also like to thank the Addison Wesley Longman staff for their support and their valuable advice throughout the development of the project. In particular, we wish to acknowledge Dugie Cameron, Michael Boyd, Barton Armstrong, Jeremy Osborne, Chris Balderston, J.J. Lee, and Betty Teng.

We would like to thank the following individuals and organizations who kindly supplied us with information and permissions to utilize copyrighted material: Victorinox and Swiss Army Brands Ltd. for permission to reproduce the photograph on page 68; *CUPS: The Cafe Culture Magazine* for information on coffee shops; Graphic-Sha Publishing Company for permission to reproduce illustrations from *Roots of Street Style* by Zeshu Takamura, ©1997 by Graphic-Sha Publishing Company and Zeshu Takamura; *The Village Voice*; the New York City Police Department; the *Guinness Book of World Records*, and Safeway Supermarkets Inc.

CONTENTS

UNIT		GRAMMAR TARGETS	FUNCTIONS	VOCABULARY FOCUS	PAGE
1	**New People**	questions with *be*: *What's your name?* *Who is she?*	introducing *Hi. I'm...*	relationships	8
2	**International Life**	questions with *does*: *Where does it come from?*	describing *It's a kind of...* asking for/ giving opinions *What's it like?*	nationality food	12
3	**Personal Information**	questions with *be* and *does*: *Where do you live?* *What's your address?*	asking for personal information *Can I ask you some questions?*	addresses phone numbers	16
4	**Impressions**	singular-plural *That's...* *Those are...* possessives *Ted's shoes*	complimenting *That's a nice...* giving opinions *They look good.*	clothing appearance	20
FLUENCY UNIT		Wh- questions review	functions review	topics review	24
5	**Interests**	negatives *He isn't...* *They aren't...* verb combinations *He likes to play...*	asking about personal interests *What do you do in your free time?*	interests free-time activities	26
6	**Shopping**	some-any *Do you have any...?* dummy subjects *There is...* *There are...*	asking prices *How much is it?*	prices products shopping	30
7	**Weekends**	past tense *What did you...?* *I went to...*	asking about/ talking about past activities *What did you do on Saturday?*	leisure activities time expressions	34
8	**Home**	adjectives and modifiers *It's kind of messy.* prepositions *It's on the bed.*	asking about conditions *What's it like?* describing *It has a lot of...*	locations personal items	38
9	**Abilities**	modals *Can you...?* *She can't...*	asking about abilities *Can you do that?*	activities	42
FLUENCY UNIT		tag questions	functions review	topics review	46

UNIT		GRAMMAR TARGETS	FUNCTIONS	VOCABULARY FOCUS	PAGE
10	Family	adverbs of frequency *He never goes out.* adjectives and modifiers *He's very nice.*	describing people *They're a little unusual.* giving examples *She complains a lot.*	personality	48
11	Places Around Town	prepositions *It's across from the bank.* imperatives *Turn left at Elm Street.*	asking directions *How do you get to the train station?*	shops places in a city	52
12	Personal Description	relative clauses (reduced) *He's the man (who's) wearing the blue suit.*	identifying someone *Is he the guy sitting in the corner?*	clothing physical features	56
13	Entertainment	noun modifiers *It's a good place to eat.* modals *I can't go. I have to...*	inviting *Would you like to...?* giving excuses *I'm sorry. I can't.*	entertainment activities frequency expressions	60
FLUENCY UNIT		present progressive and present perfect tenses	functions review	topics review	64
14	Personal Items	present progressive *What are you looking for?* conjoined sentences *It's... and it has...*	describing objects *It's made of leather.* offering help *Can I help you?*	physical features of objects	66
15	Cities	comparatives *Seoul is more exciting than...*	giving opinions *I think it's...* giving reasons *It has better...*	cities weather	70
16	Jobs	verb combinations *I don't like visiting...*	giving reasons *I like it because...*	professions job responsibilities	74
17	Future Plans	future time *I'm going to go to Mexico.*	asking about plans *What are you going to do after class?* expressing hopes *I hope to ... someday.*	activities future time expressions	78
18	Customs	modals, negatives *I don't think you should...*	expressing wishes *I wish you wouldn't do that.*	customs	82
FLUENCY UNIT		present perfect and conditionals	functions review	topics review	86

		PAGE
APPENDIX: Tape Scripts		88-90
APPENDIX: Vocabulary		91-94

INTRODUCTION

Basics in Speaking: Activities for Building Conversations is a comprehensive communication course for adult students at beginning levels. Its companion book, *Strategies in Speaking: Activities for Developing Conversations,* is intended for students at an intermediate level.

The Student Book consists of 18 main units, plus 4 review units ("Fluency Units"), with an appendix containing tape scripts and a vocabulary review. There is a separate audio cassette and a **Teacher's Manual** with suggestions for classroom use and review quizzes.

THIS BOOK OFFERS

BALANCED PRACTICE

Each unit provides practice with the **component skills** needed for conversation:
* conversation functions
* selective listening
* pronunciation
* pattern practice
* free conversation
* common phrases
* vocabulary building
* communication tasks

REAL CONTENT

Each unit features **authentic conversational language, real world topics,** and **practical tasks.**

LOW-STRESS INTERACTION

Each activity sets up **easily** for pair work or group work. Activities **satisfy** learners by focusing on both **accuracy** (Conversation, Listening, Pronunciation, Practice) and **fluency** (Exchange, Small Talk, and Communication Task).

RICH VOCABULARY

The course builds up a **1,000 key word vocabulary:**
* 200 **verbs**
* 200 **adjectives**
* 50 **adverbs**
* 600 **nouns**
These words are taken from frequency lists of **spoken** English.

STRUCTURE

The course covers the most **common grammar forms** in spoken English, and integrates them with **everyday functions.**

Each of 18 main units in *Basics in Speaking* provides a series of 9 short activities to build conversation skills. The sections are designed to be ready to teach without extensive preparation. Following are some basic teaching suggestions. Detailed teaching suggestions are found in the Teacher's Manual.

GRAMMAR TARGETS
- Allow the students a few minutes to review the table on their own. Answer questions about unfamiliar words or grammar structures.
- Ask the **WARM UP** question to begin activating the grammar targets.

1 CONVERSATION
- Ask questions about the picture. Have the students respond individually or as a class.
- Have the students read the conversation and try to complete the blanks. Then listen to the tape to check.
- Have the students practice the conversation with a partner.

2 LISTENING
- Have the students look over the "missing information" before they listen.
- Then ask the students to listen to the tape and complete the information.

3 PRONUNCIATION TIP
- Read over the "how to" advice with the students and review the models.
- Then listen to the tape and have the students practice the pronunciation tip.

4 PRACTICE
- Have the students work with a partner to practice the grammar pattern.
- Review the items with the whole class.

5 EXCHANGE
- Preview the **BASIC CONVERSATION** pattern, the **COMMUNICATION TIP**, and the **BONUS** expressions with the students.
- Then have the students stand up and practice the conversation with several different classmates.

6 VOCABULARY BUILDING
- Have the students work in pairs to complete the vocabulary activity.
- Check the follow-up questions with the whole class.

7 SMALL TALK
- Read the short passage orally with the class.
- Have the students work in small groups to ask and answer the **SMALL TALK** questions.

8 COMMUNICATION TASK
- Have the students work in pairs or small groups to exchange information in order to complete the **COMMUNICATION GOAL**.
- Have the students share the outcome with the whole class.

9 GRAMMAR CHECK
- Have the students work in pairs to complete this grammar check activity.
- Check the answers with the class.

After every 4 or 5 units, there is a review unit called a "Fluency Unit." Here are some suggestions for using the **FLUENCY UNITS**:

TALKING CIRCLES
- Arrange the students in two large circles (or a similar grouping). Each student should face his or her partner and talk about the first topic for one or two minutes.
- Then the students switch partners and talk about the same topic. Repeat this for 3 or 4 partners. Then switch topics.

ROLE PLAY
- Have the students work with a partner. They choose one of the situations and prepare a dialogue.
- After each pair rehearses their dialogue, they act it out in front of the class.

1 New People

GRAMMAR TARGETS

Names						
	What **is** (What**'s**)	**your** **her** **his**	name?	**My** name **Her** name **His** name	**is** (**'s**)	Pat.
	What **are** (What**'re**)	**their**	names?	**Their** names	**are**	Pat and Dave.
Relationships	Who **is**	she? he?		She**'s** He**'s**	my my	classmate. teacher.
	Who **are**	they?		They**'re**	my	friend**s**.

WARM UP   *What's your name? What are your classmates' names?*

1 CONVERSATION

Look at the picture. *Where are they? What is happening?*

Fill in the missing words. Then listen and check your answers.

Teresa: Hi. Can I _____ here?
_{sit   stand}

Jim: Sure.

Teresa: _____ dog.
_{Nice   Fine}

Jim: Thanks. His _____ is
_{name   call}
Rusty.

Teresa: Hi, Rusty.

Jim: And _____ name's Jim.
_{I   My}

Teresa: My _____ Teresa.
_{name   name's}
Nice to _____ you.
_{meet   meeting}

Now practice the conversation.

8

2 LISTENING 📼

Listen and write the correct information.

1. Her name is L _____ .
   His name is M _____ .

   They are in the same _____ .

2. His name is A _____ .
   Her name is S _____ .

   They are at _____ .

3 PRONUNCIATION TIP 📼

HOW TO

Introduce Yourself

Your name is very important.
Stress it. Make it strong,
l-o-n-g, and clear.

Make the name long.

My
___ name's
          James

Make it strong.

Mi
I'm ___ ka

Make it clear.

Her
___ name's
          chelle
          Mi

Now say your name.

My name's _____   I'm _____

4 PRACTICE

**Look at the pictures. Take turns. Point to a person.
Ask questions. Your partner will answer.**

EXAMPLE

What's her name?
   Her name is Sarah.
Who is she?
   She's my friend.

Andy / classmate

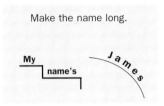

2 Sarah / friend

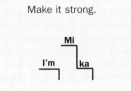

3 Kate Brock / teacher

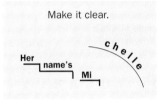

4 Brian / boyfriend

8 Mr. Sands / boss

5 Jenny and Paul / parents

7 Mark /neighbor

6 Dr. Parker / doctor

5 EXCHANGE

Stand up. Walk around the room.
Introduce yourself to your classmates.

CULTURE TIP

Make **eye contact** with your partner during the conversation. **Shake hands strongly** when you introduce yourself.

BASIC CONVERSATION

Hi, I'm _____.
    I'm _____.
Nice to meet you, _____.
    Nice to meet you too, _____.

BONUS

Try to use some of these expressions.

INTRODUCING
• Hi. my name's _____.

SAYING YOUR NAME
• My name's _____, but my friends call
  me _____.

SAYING GOODBYE
• See you later.

6 VOCABULARY BUILDING

Match the expressions on the left with the expressions on the right.

She's my friend.
She's my teacher.
She's my girlfriend.
He's my co-worker.
My name is Enrico.
They're my classmates.
He's not my boss.
He's my boyfriend.
I'm her brother.
They're our parents.

She's my sister.
I'm one of her students.
We're in the same class.
I don't work for him.
I'm Enrico.
She's a friend of mine.
We're dating.
We work together.
I go out with her.
We're their children.

Now cover the expressions on the right. Can you remember them?

7 SMALL TALK: POPULAR NAMES

Here are some popular names in the United States.
These are the "top ten" names for babies born in the U.S. in the 1990s.

Boys

1. Michael
2. Christopher
3. Matthew
4. Joshua
5. Andrew
6. James
7. John
8. Nicholas
9. Justin
10. David

Girls

1. Brittany
2. Ashley
3. Jessica
4. Amanda
5. Sarah
6. Megan
7. Caitlin
8. Samantha
9. Stephanie
10. Katherine

Talk about these questions with your classmates.

Do you know "short names" for any of these names?

What is your favorite English name?

What are some new popular names in your country?

8 COMMUNICATION TASK  Nice talking to you.

Complete this information.

- My name is ....

  My friends call me ....

- I'm interested in ....

  and ....

Now stand up. Talk to some new people. Fill in the chart.

EXAMPLE

Hi. My name is _____. What's your name?
      I'm _____.
What are you interested in?

name	interests
name	interests
name	interests
name	interests

COMMUNICATION

GOAL

*Who has the same
interests as you?*

-

9 GRAMMAR CHECK

Work with a partner. Write a question for each answer.

1. .... name?

   My name is Sandy.

2. .... Mike?

   No, it isn't. My name's Peter.

3. .... Jenny?

   She's my sister.

4. .... teacher's name?

   His name is Mr. Jordan.

5. .... ?

   No, she's not my boss.

Now practice the conversations.

2 International Life

GRAMMAR TARGETS

Asking about New Words	What is it? What is this? (What's)	It's nan.	It's **an** Indian bread. It's **a** kind of Indian bread.
Countries	Where **does** tempura come from?	It come**s** from Japan. It**'s** from Japan. It**'s** Japanese.	
	Where **do** donuts come from?	They **come** from America. They**'re** from America. They**'re** American.	
Opinions	What's **it** like?	It**'s**	good. OK.
	What are **they** like?	They**'re**	not so good.

WARM UP *What international foods do you like?*

1 CONVERSATION

Look at the picture. *Where are they? What is happening?*

Fill in the missing words. Then listen and check your answers.

Cathy: _____ this?
          What / What's

Mary: That? _____ nan.
                That / That's

Cathy: Nan? What _____ ?
                      is / is it

Mary: It's _____ Indian
              a / an
bread. _____ .
        Try / Try it

Cathy: Oh, _____ delicious.
               is / it's

Mary: I'm glad you like it.

Now **practice the conversation.**

2 LISTENING

Listen and write the correct information.

1. *Marcel and Linda are at a restaurant.*
   What is it called?
       It's called _____ .
   What is it?
       It's an _____ dessert.

2. *Marcel and Linda are at a bakery.*
   What are they called?
       They're called _____ rolls.
   What are they?
       They're a _____ pastry.

3 PRONUNCIATION TIP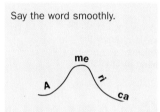

HOW TO

Say Country Names and Nationalities

Be careful. The stress in country names and nationalities often changes.

Make stressed syllables strong, l-o-n-g, and clear:

■ ■ ■ ■
America

■ = stressed syllables
■ = unstressed syllables

Jump up to the stressed syllable. Then step down.

Say the word smoothly.

Listen and repeat:

1. **Ja**pan ■ ■   You're Japa**nese**. ■ ■ ■   3. **It**aly ■ ■ ■   They're I**tal**ian ■ ■ ■
2. **Chi**na ■ ■   We're Chi**nese**. ■ ■   4. Ko**re**a ■ ■ ■   He's Ko**re**an ■ ■ ■

Now write down the name of your country and your nationality. Mark the stressed syllable. Then practice your sentences.

I'm from _____   I'm _____

4 PRACTICE

Look at the pictures. Take turns. Point to a picture. Ask questions. Your partner will answer.

EXAMPLE

What do you call this food in English?
        It's called a baguette.
What is it?
        It's a kind of bread.
        It's from France.
Oh, it's a French bread.
        That's right.

❷ FOOD • a baguette • bread • France

❸ ITEM OF CLOTHING • a sari • dress • India

❹ DRINK • vodka • liquor • Russia

❺ FOOD • macaroni • pasta • Italy

❶ SPORT • water polo • water sport • America

❻ SPORT • judo • martial art • Japan

❼ MUSIC • samba • dance music • Brazil

❽ GAME • go • a board game • China

13

5 EXCHANGE

**Stand up. Ask your classmates about these items.
Then add some new items.**

Sports	Food	Cars	Clothing	Music	New items
BASEBALL	SPAGHETTI	BMWs	BERETS	OPERA	....
POLO	KIMCHI	TOYOTAS	KIMONOS	JAZZ	

BASIC CONVERSATION

Where does _____ come from?
I think it comes from _____.
Yes, I think you're right.
OR
Are you sure?
I think it comes from _____.

BONUS

Try to use some of these expressions.

ASKING WHERE
- What country does _____ come from?
- Do you know where this comes from?

AGREEING
- I think so, too.
- Yes, right.

DISAGREEING
- I'm not sure.
- No, I don't think so.

6 VOCABULARY BUILDING

Complete this chart of countries and nationality words.

COUNTRY	NATIONALITY	COUNTRY	NATIONALITY
	Danish		French
Korea			Chinese
Britain		Russia	
	Japanese	Switzerland	
Canada			American
	Vietnamese	Turkey	

Now make five sentences using nationality words.

7 SMALL TALK: INTERNATIONAL FOODS

**In many countries you can buy food from all over the world. In a Safeway
supermarket in the States you can buy these items:**

cheese from
Holland

kiwis from
New Zealand

coffee from
Costa Rica

artichokes
from Mexico

dates
from Egypt

olive oil
from Italy

pears
from Japan

bananas from
The Philippines

pineapple
from Hawaii

Talk about these questions with your classmates.

What international foods do you buy at the supermarket?

What foods does your country export?

8 COMMUNICATION TASK — *International foods*

Think of five international foods.

Now ask your partner about the five foods.

EXAMPLE

Do you know what tiramisu is?
> *No, I don't know. What is it?*

It's _____.
> *Do you like it?*

Yes, it's good.

COMMUNICATION

GOAL

*What new foods did
you learn?*

•

How many does your partner know ? ____ / 5

9 GRAMMAR CHECK

Make sentences to match each answer.

1. _____ this comes from?
   No, I don't. Maybe it's from Brazil.

2. _____ ?
   I think it's a Hawaiian fruit.

3. _____ in English?
   It's called "salsa."

4. _____ like?
   It's good.

5. _____ macaroni is?
   It's an Italian pasta.

Now practice the conversations.

Personal Information

GRAMMAR TARGETS

Cities	Where **do** you **live**?			I	**live**	in London.
						in Taipei.
	Where **does** he **live**?			He	**lives**	in a suburb of Tokyo.
Addresses	What is	your	address?	It's		221 First Street.
				I	**live**	**at**
	What's	her	address?	She	**lives**	**at** 55 Elm Road.
		their		They	**live**	**at**
Phone Numbers	What's	your	phone number?	It's 231-0909.		
		his	home phone number?			
		their	work (business) number?			

WARM UP *What is your address, phone number, and e-mail address?*

1 CONVERSATION 📼

Look at the picture. *Where are they? What is happening?*

Fill in the missing words. Then listen and check your answers.

Officer: _____
You're   You're a

Tommy Jackson?

Timmy: Actually, my _____
first name   family name

is Timmy, sir.

Officer: And you live _____
at   in

Chicago, _____ 48 Grant Avenue?
at   in

Timmy: Actually, it's 84 Grant Avenue, sir. What's wrong, officer?

Officer: This _____ a one-
is   are

way street! Can't you _____?
spell   read

Now practice the conversation.

2 LISTENING 📼

Listen and write in the correct information.

1. Sue and Diana are going to meet at Sue's ....

   The address is ....

2. Dan is going to fax a .... to Henry.

   His fax number is ....

3 PRONUNCIATION TIP 📼

HOW TO Say Phone Numbers

Numbers have a special melody. If you use this intonation, people will understand you easily.

212 | 555 | 0793

- Group the numbers.
- Stress the last number in each group.
- Go up ⌣ at the end of each group, and then pause.
- Go down ⌢ when the last group is finished.

**Mark the stress, when to go up ⌣, when to go down ⌢ and where to pause |.
Then listen and repeat:**

1. 231-0909   2. 234-2753   3. (1) 234-6753   4. (03) 3033-5821   5. ....
                                                                        My phone number

4 PRACTICE

**Take turns. Point to a card. Ask questions about the address
or phone number. Your partner will answer.**

EXAMPLE

What is Ted Bell's address?
  *It's 311 Pine Street,
  Miami, Florida.*
What's his phone number?
  It's 305-555-0793.

Ted Bell | 311 Pine Street

Miami, Florida 33152

(305) 555-0793

ZHANG MEDICAL CENTER

Dr. Marcia Zhang, Zhang Medical Center,
510 Grant Street
San Francisco, California 94133 USA
phone: 415 - 555 - 8475

RETSU NAKAMURA

2-2-2 HONGO, BUNKYO-KU
TOKYO, JAPAN 112
PHONE: (03) 3033-5821

MS. MELINA ROYABO
CALLE 661 APT. 607E
BOGOTA, COLOMBIA
PHONE: (1) 234-27-53

COLUMBIA

M U S I C   L T D.

Mr. Martin Jones, Columbia Music Ltd.
Hampton House, Trump Sreet
London CB3 2RP, England
phone: (71)234-7800

17

5 EXCHANGE

Stand up. Talk to your classmates.
Ask their address and phone number.

BASIC CONVERSATION

Excuse me.
Can I ask you some questions?
        OK.
What is your address?
        It's _____.
What's your phone number?
        It's _____.
Thank you.

BONUS

Try to use some of these expressions.

STARTING
• Excuse me. Can I ask you a few questions?

CLARIFYING
• Pardon me?
• Could you repeat that?

REFUSING
• I'm sorry. I'd rather not say.

SPELLING
• How do you spell that?

6 VOCABULARY BUILDING

Work with a partner. Match the expressions on the left with the expressions on the right.

STREET ADDRESS
FIRST NAME
ZIP CODE
STATE OR DISTRICT

Mr. Thomas G. Smith
211 Seventh Avenue, Apartment 3-B
Portland, Oregon 84522
USA

DEPARTMENT
COUNTRY
LAST NAME
TITLE
CITY

Professor Julia Martens
English Department
University of Reading
Reading RP2 2JL
ENGLAND

COUNTRY
APARTMENT NUMBER
DISTRICT
STREET ADDRESS

Ms. Akiko Noguchi
Azabu Heights 121
1-7-19 Azabu
Shibuya-ku
Tokyo 132
JAPAN

Now write your address. Label each part.

....

....

....

7 SMALL TALK: WHO ARE YOU?

Who are you? There are many ways to identify a person. Here are some ways that are used in modern society.

- a given name
- a family name
- a nickname
- a club membership
- a passport number
- a home phone number
- an office phone number
- a fax number
- a cell phone number
- a driver's license number

- a job title
- an address
- an e-mail address
- a birth certificate
- a company affiliation
- a student ID number
- a bank account number
- a credit card number
- fingerprints

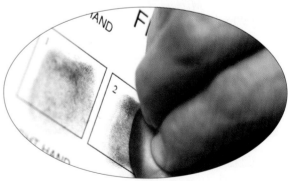

Talk about these questions with your classmates.

How many of these identities do you have?

Do you know any other ways to identify a person?

8 COMMUNICATION TASK — *It's important to me.*

Write down two important numbers and two important dates.
Don't give the reasons.

```
NUMBERS
1.
2.
```

```
DATES
1.
2.
```

Now talk to your partner. Point to a number. Ask a question.

EXAMPLE

Why is this number important?
That's my lucky number.

COMMUNICATION

GOAL

What did you learn about your partners?

•

Now switch partners. Ask again.

9 GRAMMAR CHECK

Work with a partner. Match the questions in the left column with the correct responses in the right column.

1. What is your address?
2. What's your e-mail address?
3. Where do you live?
4. Could you tell me your phone number?
5. Did you say 6641?
6. Do you live in Seoul?
7. Could you repeat that?
8. What's your phone number?
9. How do you spell that?
10. What part of the city do you live in?

a. Sure, it's 555-9822.
b. No, I live near Seoul.
c. I said 1542 H Street.
d. It's *frank@nasa.org*.
e. It's S-C-O-T-T.
f. I'd rather not say.
g. It's 551 Scott Street.
h. I live in the Richmond district.
i. At 8794 Main Street.
j. No, I said 6661.

4 Impressions

UNIT

GRAMMAR TARGETS

Compliments	I (really) like your	jacket. shoes.		Thanks. Thank you.
	That's Those **are**	a nice jacket. nice shoe**s**.		
Opinions	What do you think of	**this** Ted's	shirt? shoe**s**?	I think **it's** nice. I think **they're** great.
	Do you like	Mary's **these**	dress? shoe**s**?	No, I don't like **it**. Yes, I like **them**.
Facts	It's	new. my favorite shirt. from my mother.		
	I	**bought** **got**	it	in Thailand. at Macy's.

WARM UP *What are you wearing today?*

1 CONVERSATION

Look at the picture. *Where are they? What is happening?*

Fill in the missing words. Then listen and check your answers.

Julia: I really like _____ (that / those) sunglasses.

Paul: Oh, _____ (this / these)? _____ (It's / They're) Spectros.

Julia: They _____ (look / looks) good on you.

Paul: Thanks. I just bought _____ (it / them) yesterday.

Julia: Where _____ (do / did) you get them?

Paul: I bought them _____ (at the / at) hotel gift shop.

Now practice the conversation.

20

2 LISTENING 📟

Listen and write the correct information.

1. Jenny gives Greg a compliment about his

_____ .

He bought them in _____ .

2. Teresa compliments Janice on her

_____ .

Her _____ gave it to her.

3 PRONUNCIATION TIP 📟

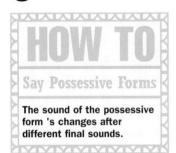

HOW TO

Say Possessive Forms

The sound of the possessive form 's changes after different final sounds.

Say /s/ for these final sounds. Make the vowel sound before /s/ quick.

/p/	Chip's
/f/	Ralph's
/k/	Mike's
/t/	Pete's
/θ/	Beth's

Say /z/ for these final sounds. Make the vowel sound before /z/ l-o-n-g.

/b/	Bob's
/d/	Ted's
/g/	Doug's
/l/	Bill's
/m/	Tom's
/n/	Dan's
/ng/	Ming's
/v/	Dave's
/vowel/	Emma's

Say /əz/ for these final sounds. This makes a new syllable.

/s/	Chris's
/z/	Rose's
/ch/	Rich's
/j/	George's
/sh/	Josh's

Listen. Check (✔) the sound you hear. Then repeat.

	Mary's	Doris's	Nicole's	Liz's	Ruth's
/s/					
/z/					
/əz/ + Extra Syllable					

4 PRACTICE

Look at the pictures. Take turns. Point to a person. Ask questions. Your partner will answer.

great   nice   neat   beautiful   wild   stylish   sporty
trendy   lovely   casual   ugly   weird   awful   unusual

EXAMPLE

What do you think of Pete's shirt?
I think it's ....

David

Tracy

Pete

Nicole

5 EXCHANGE

Look at your classmates.
Imagine compliments you can give.
Now stand up. Walk around the room. Talk to
your classmates. Give a compliment to each person.

CULTURE TIP

Smile when you give a compliment. Accept compliments by saying, **"Thank you."**

BASIC CONVERSATION

That's a nice _____.
> *Thank you. I bought it at*
> *Isetan Department Store.*

BONUS

Try to use some of these expressions.

COMPLIMENTING
• Nice vest. /Cool shoes.
• That jacket looks good on you.

ASKING
• Where did you get it?
• Is that a new suit?

RESPONDING
• It's a gift from my mother.
• My dad gave it to me.

6 VOCABULARY BUILDING

Match the items of clothing with the description.

sunglasses   You wear them on your hands.
a raincoat   You wear it around your neck.
a necklace   You wear it in cold weather.
gloves   You wear them on sunny days.
a coat   You wear it on rainy days.

shoes   You wear them on your feet.
a bracelet   You wear it around your wrist.
earrings   You wear it around your collar.
a tie   You wear them on your legs.
stockings   You wear them in your ears.

Now think of three more items of clothing. Give a description.

7 SMALL TALK: CLOTHING FADS

Every country has clothing fads. Most clothing fads last for three to five years, but some last much longer. Many clothing fads come back again and again. Can you match these clothing fads with their names and dates?

1 Garconne style, Paris, 1920s
2 Duke style, London, 1930s
3 Chanel style, Paris, 1955
4 James Dean style, USA, 1950s
5 Campus style, USA, 1950s

6 Monterey style, USA, 1965
7 Punk Rocker style, London, 1975
8 Preppie style, Boston, 1980
9 Thrasher style, Los Angeles, 1985
10 Body conscious style, London, 1990

Talk about these questions with your classmates.

Which of these fads do you like?

Which ones don't you like?

What are some fashion trends now?

8 COMMUNICATION TASK   *What are they wearing?*

Work with a partner. List five clothing items and accessories you see in the classroom. List each item only one time.

clothing item or accessory	color or style	who's wearing it
•		
•		
•		
•		
•		

COMMUNICATION

GOAL

Which items of clothing or accessories do you like the most? Why?

Now one partner closes his or her eyes. Can you remember?

EXAMPLE

Who's wearing _____?
  Kimi is./I don't remember.

9 GRAMMAR CHECK

Work with a partner. Put the words in correct order to make sentences. There is one extra word in each line.

1. like your I really you shoes. _____
2. does he what think of that dress your _____
3. nice a Pete jeans has. _____
4. did get where you are it? _____
5. you on looks that good is jacket. _____
6. do think is Paul's shirt what of you? _____
7. nice is think it's I. _____
8. got it the have States in I. _____
9. gift it's a my from the mother. _____
10. a it a lot like I. _____

ACTIVITY 1 SPEAKING CIRCLES

WH-QUESTIONS	GRAMMAR TARGETS	
Who	**Who is sitting** next to you?	**Frank is sitting** next to me.
What	**What is** your name?	My name **is Liz**.
Where	**Where do** you live?	I live in **Miami**.
When	**When does** this class start?	This class starts **at 10:00**.
Why	**Why do you** want to learn English?	I **want to work in the U.S.**
Which	**Which one** do you like?	I like **the blue one**.

❶ Sit in two rows. Face each other.
❷ Start with TOPIC 1.
❸ Talk to your partner for 1 minute.
❹ Then change partners.
❺ Talk for 1 minute about the same topic.
❻ Continue for 3 or 4 partners.
❼ Start again on TOPIC 2 with a new partner.

CULTURE TIP

Don't worry about making mistakes. Keep talking.

TOPIC 1

INTERESTS

Sample questions:
What are you interested in?
Why do you like it?
Do you like...?
Where do you do that?

TOPIC 3

FOOD

Sample questions:
Are you a good cook?
What kinds of food do you like?
What kinds of food don't you like?
What's your favorite restaurant?

TOPIC 2

PERSONAL INFORMATION

Sample questions:
Where do you live?
Do you like your place?
What's it like?
Who do you live with?

TOPIC 4

CLOTHES

Sample questions:
Where do you buy your clothes?
Do you wear accessories?
When do you usually go shopping?
Which store is your favorite?

ACTIVITY 2 ROLE PLAY

**Work with a partner. Choose a situation. Make up a dialogue.
Practice your dialogue. Then say your dialogue in front of the class.**

EXAMPLE

Two classmates meeting for the first time.

Rebecca: Hi, my name is Rebecca, but please call me Becky.
Megan: *Hi, Becky. My name is Megan.*
Rebecca: Do you like this class?
Megan: *Yeah, the teacher is nice. And I'm very interested in English.*
Rebecca: Me, too.

CULTURE TIP

Don't be afraid to use your English. Try some new expressions.

SITUATION 1

Two people meet at a party.

Possible Expressions:

Hi, my name's...

Who do you know at this party?

Are you having fun?

Nice to meet you.

SITUATION 2

A customer orders food at an international restaurant.

Possible Expressions:

Can I help you?

What is...?

Where does (Pasta Nora) come from?

It's very good.

SITUATION 3

A new student registers for class.

Possible Expressions:

What's your name?

What's your address?

Can you repeat that, please?

Could you spell that for me?

SITUATION 4

Two friends meet for dinner. One friend has on a new outfit. The other has a new haircut.

Possible Expressions:

That looks fabulous on you.

Where did you get that outfit?

Thanks, I got it...

Do you like it?

GRAMMAR TARGETS

Free Time	What	**do**	you they	**do**	in	your free time?
						their
		does	she			her
Interests	I	like	**to**	**play** sports.		I like play**ing** sports.
	She	like**s**		**listen** to music.		She like**s** listen**ing** to music.
	They	like		**work** in their garden.		They like work**ing** in their garden.
	What	**are** you		interested in?		
		is she				
	I'm			**interested in**		sports (, especially volleyball).
	She**'s**					computers (, especially surfing the Web).
Negatives	I'm not			interested in		painting.
	He**'s not** / He **isn't**					playing tennis.
	We**'re not** / We **aren't**					opera.
	They**'re not** / They **aren't**					politics.

W A R M   U P   *What do you like to do in your free time?*

1 CONVERSATION 📼

Look at the picture. *Where are they? What is happening?*

Fill in the missing words. Then listen and check your answers.

Jeff: Are you _____ in
　　　　interested　interesting
camping?

Gail: Yes. I love _____ camping.
　　　　　　　　go　to go

Jeff: Where do you _____ go?
　　　　　　　　　usually　ever

Gail: A lot of places. But I
_____ like Snake Valley.
special　especially

Jeff: Yeah, I've been _____ .
　　　　　　　　　there　to there
It's ____ beautiful place.
　　a　the

Gail: We ought to go _____
　　　　　　　　each other　together
sometime.

Now practice the conversation.

2 LISTENING

Listen and write the correct information. What are they interested in?

1. Molly is interested in _____ ,
especially _____ .

2. Lisa and Brad like to _____ .
They especially like _____ .

3 PRONUNCIATION TIP 📟

Yes/No Questions: ⌣
1. Stress the most important words.

Are you <u>interested</u> in <u>cam</u>ping?

2. Go up at the end of the question.

Are you interested in camping?

WH-Questions: ⌣ ⌢
1. Jump up to the most important word.

Where do you go camping?

2. Step down to the end of the question.

Where do you go cam
                    └ ping

Listen. Mark the stressed syllables (■). Mark where your voice goes up (⌣)and down (⌢).

1. What are you interested in?
2. Are you interested in movies?
3. What do you do in your free time?
4. Do you play sports?

Listen again and then repeat.

4 PRACTICE

Look at the pictures. Take turns. Point to a person. Ask questions. Your partner will answer.

EXAMPLE

What is Shelly interested in?
She's interested in art.
What does she do in her free time?
She paints pictures.

❶ Shelley - art - paint pictures

❷ Burt - sports - watch basketball on TV

❸ Lucy - gambling - bet at the race track

❹ Mark - languages - study Chinese

❺ Ben - talking - meet with his friends

❻ Ellie - music - listen to CDs

❼ Jimmy and Johnny - games - play pool and darts at the pub

❽ Mary and Helena - fitness - do aerobics at the sports club

27

5 EXCHANGE

**Stand up. Talk to three classmates.
Ask about their interests.**

BASIC CONVERSATION

What are you interested in?
    I'm interested in _____.
What do you do in your free time?
    I _____.

BONUS

Try to use some of these expressions.

SPECIAL INTERESTS
- I'm into art, especially graphic arts.
- I enjoy all kinds of music, but my favorite is modern rock.

GUESSING
- I guess you like Jewel.
- I bet you like Eric Clapton.

RESPONDING
- Yes, I love her.
- No, I don't really like him.

6 VOCABULARY BUILDING

Work with a partner. Put the activities into one category.

- playing football
- looking at art
- watching TV
- driving a car
- playing pool
- jogging
- gardening
- singing karaoke
- bird watching
- cooking
- snowboarding
- surfing the Web

It's Not Fun   It's Difficult

It's Fun   It's Easy

Now add one more activity to each category.

7 SMALL TALK: SPECIAL INTERESTS

There are hundreds of different "interest groups" today on the Internet. People post messages to these groups to ask questions, to share their opinions, and to make friends.
Here are some examples of interest groups.

Fashion Group   Car Lovers Group
Diet Club   Bird Watchers Group
Football Watchers Group   Extreme Sports Club
Astrology Group   Shopping Club
Antique Collectors   Parents Club

Talk about these questions with your classmates.

Do you use Internet "chat groups" or "interest groups"?

What interest groups would you like to join?

8 COMMUNICATION TASK  *Interest groups*

Circle an "interest group" to join.

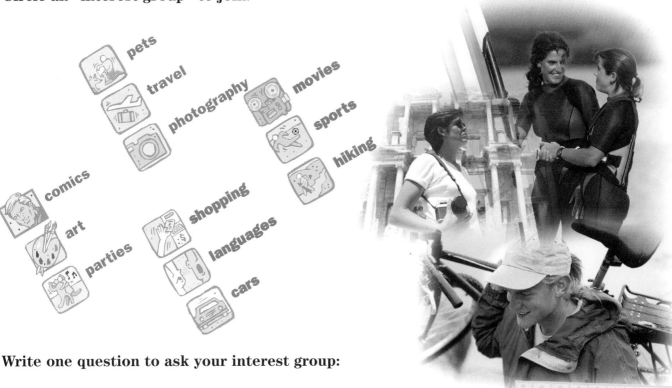

Write one question to ask your interest group:

Now stand up. Find other people in your interest group.

> **EXAMPLE**
>
> Excuse me. Are you a member of the travel interest group?
>   *Yes, I am.*
> Do you know where to buy cheap airline tickets?

*Which interest groups
have the most
members?*

  •

9 GRAMMAR CHECK

**Work with a partner. There are one or two errors in each conversation.
Correct the errors.**

1. What *do* you do in your free time?

   I like to hiking very much.

2. Do you interested in skiing?

   No, I don't interested in skiing.

3. Is he interested in movie?

   Not, no really. He don't like movies very much.

4. What do you doing in your free time?

   I like watch sports on TV.

5. Are you like movies?

   Yes, I love going the movies.

Now use the corrected sentences and practice the conversations.

6 Shopping

GRAMMAR TARGETS

Items	Do you	have sell carry	any	Godiva chocolates? Ray-Ban sunglasses?		Yes, we do. (Yes, we **have some**.) No, we don't. (No, we **don't have any**.)	
	There	**are**		**some**		over there. on the second floor.	
Prices	How much	**is**	**it**? this one?		**It's** That one is	10 dollars.	
		are	**they**? these?		**They're** Those are	99 cents.	
		does **do**	**it** **they**	cost?			

WARM UP *Do you like shopping? Where do you go shopping?*

1 CONVERSATION

Look at the picture. *Where are they? What is happening?*

Fill in the missing words. Then listen and check your answers.

Maxine: Here's _____ nice camera.
        a   the

Henry: Oh, wow! It's _____ .
          beauty   beautiful

Maxine: But _____ . It's 400
        look   see
_____ .
dollar   dollars

Henry: Oh. That's a little _____
         so   too
expensive.

Maxine: How _____ this one?
       about do you think

Henry: How _____ is it?
       many   much

Maxine: It's only 175 dollars.

Henry: Yeah, I think _____
         this one   that one
will be fine.

Maxine: OK, let's _____ .
          get   get it

Now practice the conversation.

2 LISTENING 📼

Listen and write the correct information.
What are they going to buy? What is the price?

1. Deborah   item: ....

                cost: ....

2. Max and Laura   item: ....

                         cost: ....

3 PRONUNCIATION TIP 📼

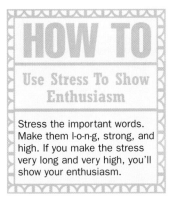

HOW TO

Use Stress To Show Enthusiasm

Stress the important words. Make them l-o-n-g, strong, and high. If you make the stress very long and very high, you'll show your enthusiasm.

Make the stressed word long.

Oh, W O W !

Make the stressed word high.

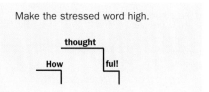

Listen. Mark the stressed syllables.

1. It's beautiful!   3. I really like it!   5. Thank you!

2. It's perfect!   4. It's very nice!

Listen again and repeat.

4 PRACTICE

Look at the pictures. Pretend you are in a shop. Take turns. Point to an item.
Ask the price. Your partner will think of a price.

> **EXAMPLE**
>
> Excuse me. I'd like to buy a watch. How much is this one?
>   *That watch is _____.*
> That's fine. I'll take it. (OR I see. I'll think about it.)

❶ an alarm clock

❻ a pair of gloves

❷ an eraser

❼ a hat

❸ a pair of sun-glasses

❽ some balloons

❹ a box of chocolates

❾ some cookies

❺ some flowers

❿ a teddy bear

5 EXCHANGE

Stand up.
Offer a "gift" to your classmates.

CULTURE TIP

Make a comment about each new topic. Be sure to contribute to the conversation. **"It's gorgeous." "It's very nice."**

BASIC CONVERSATION

Hi. I have a birthday present for you.
Oh, how thoughtful. What is it?
Here, open it.
It's perfect. Thank you so much.
You're welcome.

6 VOCABULARY BUILDING

What are these companies known for?
Match the company name with some of their products.

Company
•Nike®
•Godiva®
•Columbia®
•IBM®
•McDonalds®
•Harley Davidson®
•Coca Cola®
•Seiko®
•Sony®
•Hyundai®
•Polo®
•Gucchi®
•Avon®

Products
•automobiles
•candies
•fast food
•sports shoes
•motorcycles
•stereo equipment
•cosmetics
•CDs
•computers
•clothes
•soft drinks
•watches
•bags

What is one more product that each company produces?

7 SMALL TALK: FAMOUS SHOPPING DISTRICTS

Shopping malls became popular in the United States because people like to visit their favorite stores in one place. However, in most countries, "shopping streets" or "shopping districts" are more popular. Here are some famous shopping streets. **Do you know what cities they are in?**

• *The Ginza*
• *Peddar Street/Chater Street*
• *The Plaka*
• *5th Avenue*
• *The Rambla*
• *Kaufinger Strausse*
• *Rodeo Drive*
• *Picadilly Circus*
• *The Galleria Vittoria Emanuele*

• Hong Kong
• London
• Beverly Hills
• Tokyo
• Milan
• New York
• Munich
• Barcelona
• Athens

Talk about these questions with your classmates.

Do you know any other famous shopping areas?

What are the popular shopping areas in your city?

Complete these sentences.

EXAMPLE

What do you is the best shopping district in this city?
I think _____ is the best. How about you?

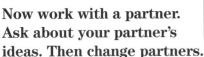

Who is the most serious shopper?

Now work with a partner. Ask about your partner's ideas. Then change partners.

1. _____ is the best shopping district in this city.

2. _____ is the best department store in this city.

3. I usually shop for clothes at _____ .

4. I go shopping about _____ times every month.

5. The last expensive thing I bought was _____ .

6. I often spend too much money on _____ .

7. I'd like to spend more money on _____ .

8. I would like to go to _____ for a "shopping holiday".

9. I am _____ with money when I
careful   not careful
go shopping.

10. I want to save money to buy a _____ .

9 GRAMMAR CHECK

Use these words to make sentences. There is one extra word in each line.

1. any do have sell you ties ?

2. we yes do some there silk any ties are second on floor the .
(two sentences)

3. do any are you carry watches Seiko ?

4. sorry don't Seiko have not watches I'm no we .
(two sentences)

5. much this watch one how is ?

6. one that dollars those is 150 .

7. that little expensive a that's it about I'll think .
(two sentences)

8. box chocolates of is this dollars 10 are ?

9. it is yes no .

10. fine that's I it take I'll .
(two sentences)

7 Weekends

GRAMMAR TARGETS

Asking General Questions	How **was** your weekend?				It **was**	OK. boring. fun.
Asking About Activities	What **did**	you Jack Amy Mike and Lisa	**do**	on Saturday? last weekend?	I He She They	**went to** a party. **watched** videos. **visited** her relatives. **saw** a movie.
	Did	you	**go** to the movies?		Yes, I No, I	**did.** **didn't.**
Opinions	I	**had**	a nice time.			
	It	**was**	an exciting movie.			

WARM UP *What did you do last weekend?*

1 CONVERSATION 🔊

Look at the picture. *Where are they? What is happening?*

Fill in the missing words. Then listen and check your answers.

Susan: How _____ your
            is   was
weekend?

Jill: Great.

Susan: What _____?
                you did did you do

Jill: I _____ a date on
          have   had
Saturday night.

Susan: Oh?

Jill: And I _____ to
          went was going
the beach on Sunday.

Susan: I'm jealous. I _____
                        went didn't go
anywhere. I _____ at
            was   did
home all weekend.

Now practice the conversation.

2 LISTENING 📟

Listen and write the correct information. What did they do on the weekend?

1. Brad

Place: ....

Activity: ....

2. Margie and Ted

Place: ....

Activity: ....

3 PRONUNCIATION TIP 📟

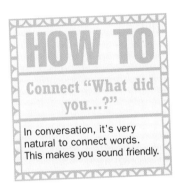

HOW TO

Connect "What did you...?"

In conversation, it's very natural to connect words. This makes you sound friendly.

Connect the sounds:

What did you	→	*Whajə**		Where did you	→	*Wherejə**
Who did you	→	*Whojə**		Why did you	→	*Whyjə**
When did you	→	*Whenjə**		How did you	→	*Howjə**

Listen and repeat. Say the WH phrases smoothly and quietly:

1. *Whajə*
   Whajə do
   Whajə do last weekend?

2. *Whojə*
   Whojə have a
   Whojə have a date with?

3. *Whenjə*
   Whenjə get
   Whenjə get home?

4. *Wherejə*
   Wherejə go?

5. *Whyjə*
   Whyjə stay
   Whyjə stay home?

6. *Howjə*
   Howjə get
   Howjə get there?

*This is not normal spelling. These forms are not in the dictionary.

4 PRACTICE

**Look at the pictures. Take turns. Point to a person. Ask questions.
Your partner will answer.**

EXAMPLE

What did Tim do last Saturday?
He had a lot of fun.
He went out to eat
with his friends.

❷ Tim • last Saturday
• have a lot of fun
• go out to eat with his friends

❸ Peter • last weekend
• have a terrible time
• break his leg skiing on Saturday

❶ Mr. and Mrs. Miller • Sunday
• have a relaxing time
• work in the garden

❹ Milly • on Friday night
• have a relaxing time
• watch a video at home

❻ Jon • Saturday
• have a hard time
• babysit for his two nieces

❺ Trudy • Saturday night
• have a boring time
• wash her clothes and clean her apartment

❼ Alice • this weekend
• have a typical weekend
• study at the library

5 EXCHANGE

Stand up. Ask your classmates about their activities last weekend.

CULTURE TIP

Ask more questions. This keeps the conversation going.
"Where did you go?"
"What was it like?"

BASIC CONVERSATION

How was your weekend?
It was OK.
What did you do on Friday night?
I stayed at home.

BONUS

Try to use some of these expressions.

ASKING
• Did you have fun last weekend?
• Was your weekend relaxing?

RESPONDING
• Saturday was pretty good, but Sunday wasn't so interesting.

REVERSING THE QUESTION
• How about you?
• Tell me what you did.

6 VOCABULARY BUILDING

Put these "past expressions" in time order.

1. yesterday
2. about the time my father was born
3. an hour ago
4. at 2 a.m. today
5. on my last birthday
6. before I was born
7. last week

10 years ago

8. a month ago
9. in 1995
10. 70 years ago
11. the year I was born
12. the day before yesterday
13. last winter
14. just a minute ago
15. last night

Now make 5 sentences with these expressions.

7 SMALL TALK: LONGER WEEKENDS

Many people say, "There's nothing to do on the weekend." Here is a recent list of activities from a "Weekend Guide."

- antique market
- comedy show
- art gallery
- photography exhibit
- dance lessons
- baseball game
- dance club
- lecture
- rock concert
- walking tour of the city
- museum exhibit
- dog show
- magic show
- symphony
- cultural festival

Talk about these questions with your classmates.

Which of these activities are interesting to you?

What kinds of weekend activities are there in your area?

8 COMMUNICATION TASK

Write down three activities you did last weekend.
Now write down one activity that you did not do last weekend.

an activity you did last weekend	an activity you did last weekend	an activity you did last weekend	an activity you didn't do last weekend

Work in a group of 4. Read your four
sentences. Can you fool your partners?

EXAMPLE

I had a date on Friday night...I got married in Las Vegas
on Saturday night...I cleaned my room for two hours on
Saturday...I went hiking on Sunday.
   I don't think you got married.
OK...you're right.

COMMUNICATION

GOAL

*What surprised you
the most?*

•

9 GRAMMAR CHECK

Using the clues given make correct sentences in the past tense.

1. Wendy   last Monday   to New York   drive

2. yesterday   buy   Fred and Kelly   a new car

3. an exam   Bill   take   the day before yesterday

4. I   in 1992   from high school   graduate

5. give   she   George   on Valentine's Day   a box of chocolates

6. the new song   hear   we   just a minute ago

7. before I was born   live   in New York   my parents

8. you   to the library   last night   not go

9. not go to the party   last Saturday   Pam and Stanley

10. not go skiing   last weekend   Margie and I   because   there is   no snow

8 Home

GRAMMAR TARGETS

Location	Where	**do**	you they	**live?**		I **live** in Northbrook. They **live** near here.
	Where	**does**	she			She **lives** downtown.
Asking Description Questions	What's	your Tom's their	apartment house place	**like?**		
Describing	Tom's My Their	apartment **is**	(kind of) (sort of) (a bit)	**nice.** **messy.** **crowded.**		
	Our Her His	place	**has** a lot of	beautiful **plants.** nice **furniture.** modern **paintings.**		

WARM UP *Where do you live? Do you like your apartment or house?*

1 CONVERSATION

Look at the picture. *Where are they? What is happening?*

Fill in the missing words. Then listen and check your answers.

Janie: Where's apartment 301? Oh, _____ !
<u>it is there</u>   <u>there it is</u>

Matt: Hi, Janie.

Janie: Hi, Matt. Oh, _____ <u>my</u> <u>your</u> apartment is _____ nice.
<u>a little</u> <u>very</u>

Matt: Really? I think it's _____ small.
<u>kind</u> <u>kind of</u>

Janie: No, it's perfect. I _____ like it.
<u>very</u> <u>really</u>

Matt: Oh, thanks. Well, _____ <u>go</u> <u>come</u> in. Make yourself at home.

Now practice the conversation.

38

2 LISTENING

Listen and write the correct information. What is each place like?

1. Karen's apartment

   • ....

   • ....

2. Marco's room

   • ....

   • ....

3 PRONUNCIATION TIP

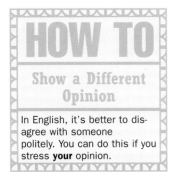

HOW TO

Show a Different Opinion

In English, it's better to disagree with someone politely. You can do this if you stress **your** opinion.

Go up on the question.

Really?

Then stress "I" and how you **really** feel:

I think it's **small**.

Listen. Mark the stressed syllables (■). Mark where to go up (‿).

1. A: This apartment is terrible.
   B: Really? I think it's nice.

2. A: This place is great.
   B: Do you think so? I think it's a little crowded.

3. A: This place is too small.
   B: Oh? I think it's cozy.

Listen again and repeat.

4 PRACTICE

Look at the pictures. Take turns. Point to a place.
Ask about the place. Your partner will answer. Then disagree.

EXAMPLE

Do you like Tony's house?
Yes, I think his place is interesting.
Really? I think it's kind of boring.

❶ Ken's place
• is luxurious • is junky

❷ Mika's house
• is beautiful • is a little old-fashioned

❸ Tony's house
• is interesting • is messy

❹ Amy's room
• comfortable • is crowded

❺ Larry's room
• is in a lively neighborhood • is in a noisy neighborhood

❻ Tom and Jen's apartment
• is very modern • is very weird

❼ Tina's flat • is in a nice neighborhood
• is in a snobby neighborhood

❽ Lyn's apartment
• is unique • is sort of strange

5 EXCHANGE

Stand up. Walk around the room.
Ask about your classmates' homes.

BASIC CONVERSATION

Where do you live?
  I live in _____.
What's your place like?
  It's _____.

BONUS

Try to use some of these expressions.

ASKING
• What part of (city) do you live in?
• Do you like your place?

GETTING MORE INFORMATION
• What do you like about it?
• Do you have a ____ ?
• Is there a piano in your house?

ANSWERING
• There's a lot of nice furniture in my house.
• I live in a really quiet part of town.

6 VOCABULARY BUILDING

Say where each item is: *the cat, the guitar, the broom, the magazines, the toaster, the dishes, the leftover food. Example: The cat is on the couch.* Try to use these expressions:

on   in   under   between   over   beneath   above   beside   next to   near

What other objects are in the room?

7 SMALL TALK: HOTELS

Here are the names of some of the world's largest hotels.

1. MGM Grand, 5,012 rooms
2. Excalibur, 4,032 rooms
3. Hilton Flamingo, 3,530 rooms
4. Mirage, 3,049 rooms
5. Treasure Island, 2,900 rooms
6. Hilton, 2,877 rooms
7. Bally Grand Hotel, 2,832 rooms
8. Circus Circus, 2,793 rooms
9. Imperial Palace, 2,637 rooms
10. Lumor Hotel, 2,533 rooms

All of these hotels are in the same city. Can you guess which city?

(a) New York   (b) Tokyo   (c) Las Vegas   (d) Hong Kong

Talk about these questions with your classmates.

What's the largest hotel in your country?

Do you like to stay in hotels? Why or why not?

Imagine: You are going to stay in a hotel room for one month.
Design your room. Include doors, windows, furniture, decorations.

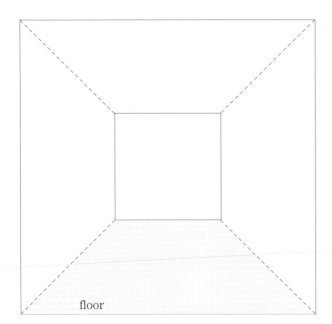

floor

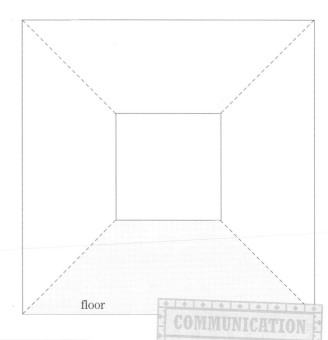

floor

Work with a partner. Ask questions. Draw a picture of your partner's hotel room. (Don't look at your partner's picture!)

EXAMPLE

Do you have a bed?
Yes.
Where is it?
It's...

COMMUNICATION GOAL

Share your room pictures with the class. Whose hotel room is the most interesting?

•

9 GRAMMAR CHECK

Fill in the sentences with the correct possessive form.

I	you	he	she	it	we	they
my	your	his	her	its	our	their
mine	yours	his	hers		ours	theirs

1. I know Tom. That's _____ condo. He has lived there for five years.

2. Beth invited me to _____ house. _____ address is 2020 Prentice Road.

3. We love _____ new duplex. It's perfect!

4. My neighbors are the Katos. _____ apartment is next to _____.

5. Meg lives in a small apartment. It is expensive, but she likes _____ location.

6. Mary, let's go back to _____ hotel room. We need to pack our suitcases.

7. My dog Muff has _____ own house. It sleeps there most nights, but sometimes it

   sleeps in _____ bed with me.

8. Sam, I love this apartment. Is it _____?

9. We like our new place, but _____ neighbors are very loud.

GRAMMAR TARGETS

Abilities	Can	you she they	**speak** French? **swim?**		Yes, **I can**. / No, **I can't**. Yes, **she can**. / No, **she can't**. Yes, **they can**./ No, **they can't**.	
Reasons	I He	**can** **can**	**speak** French. **swim**.	I He	**lived** in Paris **learned** how to swim	**for** two years. **when** he was a child.
	She They	**can't** **can't**	**dance**. **sing**.	She's They're not	very very	clumsy. musical.
Degrees	They He	**are** **is**	great really good pretty good not very good sort of bad terrible		**at** tennis. **at** ice skating.	

WARM UP *What are five things you can do? What are five things you can't do?*

1 CONVERSATION 🔊

Look at the picture. *Where are they? What is happening?*

Fill in the missing words. Then listen and check your answers.

Jim: Do you _____ go with _____ ?

want   want to

we   us

Sue: Where are you _____ ?

go   going

Jim: _____ karaoke bar.

To   To a

Sue: Oh, gosh, no. I _____ sing karaoke.

can   can't

Jim: What? Everybody can _____ karaoke.

sing   sings

Sue: No, really, I can't. It's _____ . I'm a terrible _____ .

possible   impossible

song   singer

Jim: Oh, come on. _____ you some easy songs.

I teach   I'll teach

Now practice the conversation.

2 LISTENING 📟

Listen and write the correct information. What can or can't they do? Why?

1. Kyle can't .... 2. Laura can ....

   because ....   because ....

3 PRONUNCIATION TIP 📟

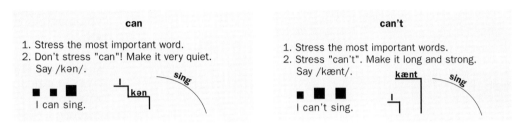

HOW TO

Say "can" and "can't"

It's important to make a big difference between these two words. The secret is in stress and intonation.

can

1. Stress the most important word.
2. Don't stress "can"! Make it very quiet. Say /kən/.

■ ■ ■   I can sing.

can't

1. Stress the most important words.
2. Stress "can't". Make it long and strong. Say /kænt/.

■ ■ ■   I can't sing.

Listen. Do you hear "can" or "can't"? Check the word you hear.

	can	can't	Sentence
1.			
2.			
3.			

	can	can't	Sentence
4.			
5.			

Listen again and write the sentence. Mark the stressed syllables. Then repeat.

4 PRACTICE

**Look at the pictures. Take turns. Point to a person. Ask questions.
Your partner will answer.**

EXAMPLE

Can Shelly draw?
  No, she can't. She's not very good at it.

❶ Su-Lyn
• can't speak English well
• is very shy

❷ Ellen • can ski
• always goes on the hardest hills

❸ Larry • can go hiking
• has strong legs

❹ Shelly • can't draw
• isn't very good at it

❺ Burt • can play baseball
• is very athletic

❻ Helena • can't do aerobics • is a little lazy

❼ Mike • can't dance
• feels embarrassed

❽ Bobby • can't roller-skate • can't keep his balance

❾ Ellie • can build things with her Lego blocks
• is very creative

❿ Ziggy • can't play a musical instrument
• can't read music

43

5 EXCHANGE

**Stand up. Talk to your classmates.
Ask about their abilities.**

CULTURE TIP

Use a sense of humor. This makes the conversation more friendly.
"Really? You can't!?"

BASIC CONVERSATION

Can you _____?
    Yes, I can. I _____.
    OR
    No, I can't. I _____.

BONUS

Try to use some of these expressions.

ASKING
• Are you good at (skiing)?
• How well can you (ski)?

ANSWERING
• I can do that pretty well.
• I know how to do that a little bit.
• No, I never learned how to do that.

AGREEING WITH...

(YES, I CAN.)	(NO, I CAN'T.)
• Me, too.	• Me, neither.
• So can I.	• I can't, either.
• I can, too.	

6 VOCABULARY BUILDING

Match the statement on the left with a statement on the right.

Janice can sing a lot of karaoke songs well.
Jack can lift 200 kilograms.
Gwen doesn't speak English very well.
Rachel always gets the lead part in the school plays.
Lisa can read Chinese fluently.
Leon can play a bunch of different sports.
Martha gets tired when she does aerobics.
Brett can't drive.
Amy can't climb mountains.
Sam doesn't play baseball very well.
The Spartans will win the championship this year.
Kenny plays the guitar really well.

She's an excellent actor.
She's afraid of heights.
She grew up in Hong Kong.
She's not in very good shape.
He took lessons from Eric Clapton!
He's very strong.
His parents won't allow him to take the driving test.
He's very athletic.
He can't catch the ball.
They can beat every team in the league.
She's shy about practicing her English.
She has a nice voice.

Can you make one new pair of sentences?

7 SMALL TALK: GUINNESS BOOK OF WORLD RECORDS

The Guinness Book Of World Records lists many individual records, such as :

- pogo-stick jumping (177,737 times in a row)
- eating eggs (17 in 20 seconds)
- kissing (8,001 people in 8 hours)
- standing (17 years)
- typing (216 words a minute)
- stone skipping (38 skips)
- basketball spinning (18 balls at one time)

Talk about these questions with your classmates.

Have you heard of any unusual records like these?

Do you have any special abilities?

How could you get into The Guinness Book of World Records?

Work with a partner. Which activities can you do? Which can your partner do?
Write your initials and your partner's initials next to each one you can do.

.... do magic tricks
.... speak English very well
.... drive a car
.... ride a bicycle
.... stand on one leg for 10 seconds
.... swim
.... drive a motorcycle
.... rollerskate

.... say "hello" in five languages
.... understand this problem:
.... $y = ax + b$
.... catch a football
.... play the guitar
.... sing karaoke
.... dance
.... speak a little French
.... play chess
.... ski
.... tell a joke in English
.... play poker
.... read Chinese
.... remember your 1st grade teacher's name

COMMUNICATION

GOAL

Who in your class has special abilities?

•

EXAMPLE

Can you drive a car?
   Sure. I can do that.
How about drive a motorcycle?
   No, I can't.

Now think of one more activity that you both can do. Share your answers with the class.

9 GRAMMAR CHECK

Work with a partner. There are one or two errors in each conversation.
Correct the errors.

1. Can Alan plays tennis?
   Yes, he can, but he's not very good at.

2. Can Lisa to do aerobics?
   No, she isn't. She's a little lazy.

3. Are you a good skier?
   No, not really. I always falling down.

4. How well Jerry can ski?
   Very well. He's an excellent skier.

5. Why you can't go snowboarding with us?
   I have weak knees. I can't to snowboard.

6. Are you good at speaking English?
   No, I'm not.
   Me, too.

Now use the corrected sentences and practice the conversations.

ACTIVITY 1 SPEAKING CIRCLES

TAG QUESTIONS GRAMMAR TARGETS	
Statement	**Yes, that's correct. =**
You are interested in baseball, aren't you? This is my hamburger, isn't it?	Yes, I am. Yes, it is.
They live in Canada, don't they? Paul speaks Korean, doesn't he?	Yes, they do. Yes, he does.
We aren't going to the park, are we? Mary isn't interested in jazz, is she?	No, we aren't. No, she isn't.
Your house doesn't have a lot of plants, does it? Tom and Jan don't like Thai food, do they?	No, it doesn't. No, they don't.
You can swim, can't you? Sue can't sing very well, can she?	Yes, I can. No, she can't.

❶ Sit in two rows. Face each other.
❷ Start with TOPIC 1.
❸ Talk to your partner for 1 minute.
❹ Then change partners.
❺ Talk for 1 minute about the same topic.
❻ Continue for 3 or 4 partners.
❼ Start again on TOPIC 2 with a new partner.

CULTURE TIP

Don't be afraid to give your opinion. Say your own ideas.

TOPIC 1

INTERESTS

Sample questions:
What do you do in your free time?
Where do you like to...?
Why do you enjoy doing that?

TOPIC 2

SHOPPING

Sample questions:
Do you like...?
Where do you usually...?
How much do you...?

TOPIC 3

WEEKENDS

Sample questions:
What did you do last weekend?
Did you see a movie last weekend?
Where did you go last weekend?

TOPIC 4

HOME

Sample questions:
What is your place like?
Why do you like your house?
What don't you like about your home?
You live with your parents, don't you?

TOPIC 5

ABILITIES

Sample questions:
Do you like to...?
You can do that well, can't you?
Why do you like to do that?
Where did you learn how to do that?

ACTIVITY 2 ROLE PLAY

Work with a partner. Choose a situation. Make up a dialogue.
Practice your dialogue. Then say your dialogue in front of the class.

EXAMPLE

Two college roommates talking about their classes.

George: I'm having trouble in English class.
Richard: Why?
George: I can't understand very much. The teacher talks too fast.
Richard: Did you talk to the teacher about it?

CULTURE TIP

Don't be afraid to use your English. Try some new expressions.

SITUATION 1

A customer and a clerk are in a department store.

Possible Expressions:

Can I help you?

I'm looking for...

How much money do you want to spend?

You take credit cards, don't you?

SITUATION 2

An English student is talking to the English teacher.

Possible Expressions:

I get too nervous in class, so I can't...

I have a hard time with...

You practice speaking English outside of class, don't you?

Why don't you try...

SITUATION 3

Two friends are talking about their past weekend. One had a super weekend; one had a very boring weekend.

Possible Expressions:

What did you do?

Did you do anything besides watch TV?

I'm so jealous!

You had an exciting weekend, didn't you?

SITUATION 4

Two acquaintances are talking before a business meeting.

Possible Expressions:

Do you like working for this company?

What do you like to do on the weekends?

I love to surf. What about you?

SITUATION 5

A couple are deciding how to decorate their apartment.

Possible Expressions:

Do you want to paint the walls?

I think we should...

What about....?

You don't think that is a good idea, do you?

47

10 Family

GRAMMAR TARGETS

Asking about People	What's What **are**	your wife your parents	like?	
Describing with Adjectives	He's She's They're	very really kind of a little	nice. smart. mean. boring.	
Describing with Examples	He They	likes like	meeting people. to meet people. spending time outdoors. to spend time outdoors.	
	She	never always	tries new things. gets angry.	

WARM UP *Can you describe one person in your family?*

1 CONVERSATION

Look at the picture. *Where are they? What is happening?*

Fill in the missing words. Then listen and check your answers.

Beth: Are these your _____?
                           parents   relatives

Alan: Yeah, that was last year at my _____
              promotion   graduation

Beth: What's your _____ like?
                        dad   mom

Alan: My father? He's very _____.
                              tradition   traditional

Beth: How _____ your mother?
              is   about
What's she _____?
           like   likes

Alan: She's very easy-going.
She gets _____ with everyone.
         around   along

Beth: Hmm. I'd like to meet them _____.
         sometime   sometimes

Now practice the conversation.

2 LISTENING 📟

Listen. Describe each person. Use one word or phrase, plus an example.

1. Lyn's mother is ....

   Example: ....

2. Lyn's father is ....

   Example: ....

3 PRONUNCIATION TIP 📟

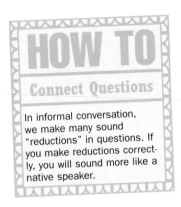

HOW TO

Connect Questions

In informal conversation, we make many sound "reductions" in questions. If you make reductions correctly, you will sound more like a native speaker.

"What are...?"

Drop the "a" in "are". Change "t" to "d".
Whad er your **pa**rents like?

"What's your... ?"

Make a new sound: "ch".
*Whacher** **fa**ther like?

*Say "Whacher...?" Write "What's your...?"

"What's he.... ?"

Drop the "h" in "he".
What's e like?

"What's she.... ?"

Drop the "s" in "What's".
What she like?

Listen. Mark the stressed syllables. Mark the sound changes in the word connections.

1. What's your mother like?
2. What's she like?
3. What's your brother like?
4. What's he like?
5. What are your grandparents like?
6. What are they like?

Listen again and repeat. Say each question in one breath.

4 PRACTICE

Look at the pictures. Take turns. Point to a person.
Ask questions about Amy's family. Your partner will answer.

EXAMPLE

Who's that?
   That's Amy's mother.
Amy's mother? What's she like?
   She's very active.
Really?
   Yes, she goes out a lot.

❺ grandparents
annoying
complain all the time

❼ brothers
nice
easy to get along with

❾ cousin
clumsy
always breaks things

❶ mother
active
goes out a lot

❸ father
a little dull
never goes anywhere

❷ dog
boring
only stays at home

❹ cat
interesting
does a lot of fun things

❻ uncle
crazy
tries lots of dangerous stuff

❽ aunt
stubborn
never changes her mind

❿ older sister
funny
laughs a lot

49

5 EXCHANGE

Draw a family tree. Write the names of your family members.

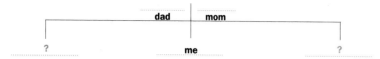

dad | mom

? | me | ?

Now stand up.
Look at your classmates' names.
Ask questions about them.

BASIC CONVERSATION

Who is that?
    That's my _____.
What's she like?
    She's _____.

BONUS

Try to use some of these expressions.

ASKING
• Is (your dad) very serious?
• What does your brother do?

GETTING MORE INFORMATION
• Why do you say that?
• What do you mean?

CONTINUING THE CONVERSATION
• (My mother) is like that too.
• I know what you mean.

6 VOCABULARY BUILDING

Work with a partner. Match the expressions.

She has interesting hobbies.
He's funny.
She's stubborn.
He's a little mean.
She's really nice.
He's exciting.
She's very strict.
He's boring.
She's not so adventurous.
He's very outgoing.

He likes to tell jokes. He makes me laugh.
He has a lot of interesting ideas.
She makes a lot of rules for us.
He often gets angry.
He doesn't like to try new stuff.
He talks to everyone.
She loves to dance, shop, and collect comics.
She never changes her mind.
She's very comfortable to be around.
She just stays home most of the time.

Now make a new pair of sentences.

7 SMALL TALK: LEARNING FROM OUR FAMILY

Twenty-four international students at the University of California were asked: What values did your parents teach you? Here are some of their answers.

• Don't depend on other people to help you.
• Don't interrupt other people.
• Always be on time.
• Use money wisely.
  ("Money doesn't grow on trees.")
• Be generous.
• Bring a gift when you visit someone.
• Never tell lies.

• If you work hard, you will succeed.
• Don't embarrass other people.
• Always take care of your family first.
• Be sure to get a good education.
• Treat people equally.
• Show your gratitude to others.
  (Always say "thank you.")
• Save money. ("Save for a rainy day.")

Talk about these questions with your classmates.

What is one thing you learned from your father?

What is one thing you learned from your mother?

What is something you would like to teach your children?

8 COMMUNICATION TASK *Family topics*

Write three statements about your family. Here are some examples:

My family is happy. My grandfather/grandmother is (was) very interesting.

My family is very important to me. I like to spend my free time at home.

I like living with my family. My mother / father understands me very well

My parents are (were) very strict. My father / mother gives me good advice.

We laugh a lot in our home. My father / mother is (was) a great cook.

My father / mother works (worked) too hard. I am similar to my mother / father.

I learned a lot from my father/ mother. I like to bring my friends to my home.

We argue a lot in our home. My parents usually agree with my opinions.

Use the examples, or write your own statements:

> **EXAMPLE**
>
> My parents are very strict. Are your parents strict, too?
> *No, they aren't.*

- ....
- ....
- ....

COMMUNICATION GOAL

Which of your partner's statements is most interesting?

Work with a partner. Talk about your families.

9 GRAMMAR CHECK

Choose the correct form of the verb in each sentence.

1. My sister Lisa likes to (a) play / (b) playing sports. She hates to (a) stay / (b) staying at home.

2. My cat Bamford just (a) lying / (b) lies under the table all day. He doesn't like (a) go to outside / (b) to go outside .

3. My grandfather (a) spend / (b) spends a lot of time (a) to take / (b) taking care of his garden.

4. My mother enjoys (a) talk / (b) talking to my friends. She always (a) asks to / (b) asks them à lot of questions.

5. My father (a) comes to / (b) comes home late at night. He usually (a) goes out / (b) goes to out with his business partners after work.

6. My brother Eric (a) stays around / (b) stays up until late at night because he always (a) having / (b) has a lot of tests at the university.

7. My sister is very (a) easy-go. / (b) easy-going. She (a) gets away / (b) gets along with everyone.

8. My family (a) don't / (b) doesn't get along very well. We are always (a) argue / (b) arguing with each other.

51

11 Places Around Town

GRAMMAR TARGETS

Asking for Directions	Where is Where's			the subway station? the 42nd Street subway station? the bus stop? Central Park?
Locations	It's		on near next to across from	First Street. the bus station. the post office. the bank.
Giving Directions	**Turn**	right left	on at	Maple Drive. the church.
	Go	down straight	for	two blocks. five miles.

W A R M   U P   *Where's the closest bank? restaurant? bus stop? subway station*

1 CONVERSATION

Look at the picture. *Where are they? What is happening?*

Fill in the missing words. Then listen and check your answers.

Cindy: ....
           I'm sorry   Excuse me

Gary: Yes?

Cindy: I'm ....
           losing   lost
Where is .... ?
      subway station   the subway station

Gary: Do you ....
               have   know
Martin's Department Store?

Cindy: Yes.

Gary: It's .... same
         the   on the
street. Just go down
.... block.
one more   more one

Cindy: Great! Thank you.

Now practice the conversation.

52

2 LISTENING 📻

Listen and write the correct information. What are they looking for? Where is it?

1. He's looking for _____ .   2. She's looking for _____ .

   Location: _____ .   Location: _____ .

3 PRONUNCIATION TIP 📻

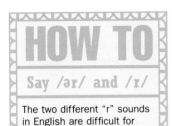

HOW TO

Say /ər/ and /r/

The two different "r" sounds in English are difficult for many non-native speakers. /r/ is a consonant sound and /ər/ is a vowel sound.

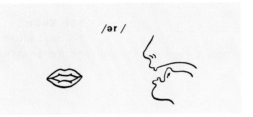

/ər/

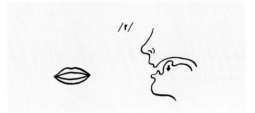

/r/

Don't let the tip of your tongue touch anything in your mouth!

Listen. Underline /ər/ when you hear it.

Example: T<u>ur</u>n **r**ight on F<u>ir</u>st St**r**eet.

1. Go st**r**aight.
2. It's on the corn**er**.
3. Just go down one mo**r**e block.
4. It's ac**r**oss f**r**om the chu**r**ch.

5. Whe**r**e's Martin's Depa**r**tment Sto**r**e?
6. T**ur**n left at the t**r**ain station.
7. It's nea**r** the G**r**een St**r**eet bus stop.

Listen again. Circle /r/ when you hear it. Then repeat.

Example: Turn ⓡight on First Stⓡeet.

4 PRACTICE

Look at the map. Take turns. Choose a place: a bank, a store, a park, a subway station, a bus stop. Ask for the location. Your partner will tell you.

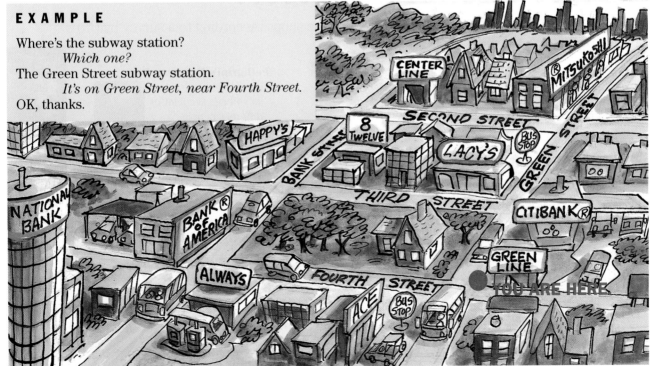

EXAMPLE

Where's the subway station?
   Which one?
The Green Street subway station.
   It's on Green Street, near Fourth Street.
OK, thanks.

53

5 EXCHANGE

Think of three places near your school: a bank,
a store, a subway station, a fast-food restaurant, etc.
Stand up. Ask your classmates for directions
to these places.

COMMUNICATION TIP

Find a common point to give directions.
"Do you know...?"

BASIC CONVERSATION

Do you know how to get to the train station?
Sure. From here,...

6 VOCABULARY BUILDING

Work with a partner. Write a name for each type of place.
Example: a fast food restaurant   McDonald's

a park ....

a bakery ....

a bank ....

a drug store ....

a coffee shop ....

a gas station ....

a music store ....

a hair salon ....

a gym ....

a grocery store ....

What other types of places are in your city?

7 SMALL TALK: COFFEE HOUSES

Melbourne, Australia is well-known for its great coffee shops. According to a survey by *Cups* magazine, here are the most popular ones.

Baker's Cafe
•It has a relaxed, casual atmosphere.
•It has a healthy menu.
•It's open until very late.

The Black Market Cafe
•It's old and dark and has a cozy atmosphere.

Pelligrini's Espresso Bar
•It's always crowded, so you can see a lot of different people.

Druids Coffee
•They have the strongest coffee in the city.

Everyday Cafe
•It has outdoor tables.
•It has a peaceful atmosphere.

Pascali's Coffee Shop
•It's a family business. (Dominic Pascali and "Mrs. P." will remember you.)
•They have nice homemade pastries.

Talk about these questions with your classmates.

What do people do in coffee shops?

Which one do you go to often?

Which coffee shop in your city is the most interesting?

8 COMMUNICATION TASK

What places do you go to often?
Write a name for each place below.

a shop ....   a coffee house ....   a restaurant ....

a park ....   a train or subway station ....   one other place ....

Now draw a very simple map of your city. Write the places on the map.

Work in a group of four. Find out about your partners' places.
Ask where they are.

EXAMPLE

I like The Black Cat Lounge.
It's a good place to meet people.
Where is it?
It's near Park Lane Station.

What new places
would you like to try?

•

9 GRAMMAR CHECK

Work with a partner. There are one or two errors in each conversation. Correct the errors.

1. Excuse me. Where's ~~a~~ *the* bus stop?

   The bus stop is on the corner.

2. Excuse me. I'm looking the Macy's
   Department Store.

   Macy's is on Fifth Avenue.

3. Excuse me. Is the subway station near here?

   No, it isn't. It's on the 42nd Street.

4. Excuse me. Do you where Ted's Camera Shop?

   Ted's Camera Shop is on Third Avenue.

5. Where is the subway station?

   I'm sorry. I don't know there.

6. Where is your apartment?

   It's on Fifth Street. It's across the bank.

7. I'm looking for the subway station.

   Which subway station you look for?

8. I'm lost. Where is Tower Records?

   Do you know Macy's? It's next it.

9. Do you know how to get to Gold's Gym?

   Sorry, I'm afraid I didn't know.

10. Do you know where the airport is?

    I think I know where is.

Now use the corrected sentences and practice the conversations.

Personal Description

GRAMMAR TARGETS

Asking Identification Questions	Which	one person	is	your boss? the teacher?		
	Which	ones	are	your friends?		
Identifying	He's She's	the man one			**with**	dark hair. blue eyes.
	They're	**the** ones wom**en**			stand**ing**	in the corner. by the door.
More Specific	He's She's	**the** man **the** person	(who **is**)		wearing	the blue tie. the black hat.
	They're	**the** men	(who **are**)		holding	the umbrellas.

WARM UP   *Think of two people in the room. Can you describe them?*

1 CONVERSATION 📟

Look at the picture. *Where are they? What is happening?*

Fill in the missing words. Then listen and check your answers.

Janet: _____ one is your fiancé?
<u>What   Which</u>

Gail: _____ tall one.
<u>A   The</u>

Janet: The tall guy _____
<u>wears   wearing</u>
a gray suit?

Gail: Yes, _____ right.
<u>you're   that's</u>

Janet: Oh, he's _____ handsome.
<u>a   very</u>

Gail: Thanks. _____ think so, too.
<u>I   you</u>

Now practice the conversation.

2 LISTENING 📻

Listen and write the correct information. How do they describe the person?

1. Jay
   Description: ....

   ....

2. Martha Swan
   Description: ....

   ....

3 PRONUNCIATION TIP 📻

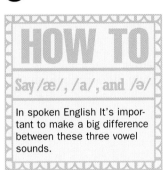

Say /æ/, /a/, and /ə/

In spoken English It's important to make a big difference between these three vowel sounds.

/æ/
A sheep makes this sound.

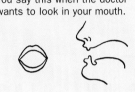

/a/
You say this when the doctor wants to look in your mouth.

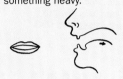

/ə/
You say this when you pick up something heavy.

Circle the sounds you hear.

1. fiancé	æ	a	ə
2. umbrella	æ	a	ə
3. the tall one	æ	a	ə
4. He's handsome.	æ	a	ə

5. That's right.	æ	a	ə
6. an attractive woman	æ	a	ə
7. dark glasses	æ	a	ə
8. the man in the hat	æ	a	ə

Listen again and repeat.

4 PRACTICE

Look at the pictures. Take turns. Choose a name. Ask about the person. Your partner will identify him or her.

EXAMPLE

Which one is Sam?
He's the man sitting by the fire.

5 EXCHANGE

Stand up. Pretend that you can't remember anyone's name! Ask your classmates to help you remember.

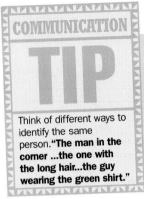

BASIC CONVERSATION

I can't remember her name.
Who are you talking about?
The woman wearing the long black dress.
Oh, that's Susie.
Oh, right. Thank you.

BONUS

Try to use some of these expressions.

ASKING FOR CLARIFICATION
• Who are you talking about?
• Is she the one wearing glasses?
• Is he the guy sitting in the corner?

IDENTIFYING
• Look — over there!
• Can't you see her?

COMMENTING
• Wow! She's gorgeous.
• He looks like a really pleasant person.

6 VOCABULARY BUILDING

Match each expression with an *opposite* expression.

Max is almost bald.	Her hair is its natural color.
I think Lucy is wearing a wig.	She's a little overweight.
Emma wears too much make-up.	He almost never wears a suit.
Len has a thick mustache and beard.	He's kind of short.
Millie has dyed her hair.	She has dark hair.
Michelle's hair is blonde.	She's got her contact lenses in.
Kay has her glasses on.	He has a lot of hair.
Mel usually dresses very formally.	He's clean shaven.
Mitch is rather tall.	That's her own hair.
Carmen is so skinny.	She doesn't like to put anything on her skin.

Can you think of one more pair of opposite expressions?

7 SMALL TALK: DISGUISES

The New York Police Department (NYPD) says that criminals often wear disguises. The department trains its officers how to recognize disguises. Here are the most common disguises.

- dyed hair
- a new hair style
- a shaved head
- a wig
- jewelry

- a hat
- glasses
- dark glasses
- false eyelashes
- false eyebrows
- false teeth

- a fake mustache
- a fake beard
- an artificial nose
- a mask
- heavy make-up

dyed hair

fake beard

Talk about these questions with your classmates.

Do you know any other disguises?

If you wanted to change your appearance, what disguise would you use?

8 COMMUNICATION TASK *Drawing lesson*

Work with a partner. First, draw a person in square #1.
Make a choice for each item:

❏ female
❏ male

1. head shape
❏ round
❏ square (wide)
❏ long (oval)

2. eyes
❏ almond-shaped
❏ round
❏ narrow

3. eyebrows
❏ bushy
❏ thick
❏ thin

4. glasses
❏ no glasses
❏ wire frame glasses
❏ dark frame glasses

5. hair
❏ thin
❏ thick
❏ straight
❏ curly wavy
❏ completely bald
❏ bald on top

6. hair length
❏ very short
❏ short
❏ medium-length
❏ shoulder-length

7. hair style
❏ slicked back
❏ hanging over
   the forehead
❏ hanging over
   the ears

8. nose
❏ small
❏ wide (broad)
❏ narrow
❏ long

9. lips
❏ thick
❏ thin

10. facial hair
❏ mustache
   (thick, thin)
❏ beard
   (thick, thin)

11. accessories
❏ hair band
❏ earrings (round,
   (triangle-shaped,...)

Then describe your drawing to your partner. **1**
(Don't show it!) Your partner will draw it.
It's OK to ask questions.
Draw your partner's picture in square #2.

2

EXAMPLE

• Does he have long hair or short hair?
• Is he wearing glasses?
• What kind of glasses?

9 GRAMMAR CHECK

Work with a partner. Put the words in correct order to make sentences.
There is one extra word in each line.

1. he's   blue   one   is   the   shoes   with.

2. which   your   who   one   boss   is?

3. with   one   he   beard   she   is   the   the   long.

4. dancing   Lois   is   the   corner   Mark   and   couple   in   the   are.

5. that's   yes   her   no.

6. the   sitting   they're   one   couch   ones   the   on.

7. man   with   hair   is   Peter   the   on   dark.

8. teacher's   book   women   the   is   holding   woman   the.

9. about   you   who   is   talking   are?

10. person   like   nice   Heather   a   looks   people.

13 Entertainment

GRAMMAR TARGETS

Asking	Would	you she they	like	to	go to Cafe Elite come to my house see a movie	tonight? next week? on Friday night?
Answering	I She We They	can't.		I She We They	have to has to have to have to	study. work.
Places	What is a good place		to	go hear	for dinner? some good jazz?	
	"The Fillmore Club"		**is a** good **place**	**to**	**go** for dinner. **hear** some good jazz.	

WARM UP   *What was the last invitation you accepted?*

1 CONVERSATION 📼

Look at the picture. *Where are they? What is happening?*

Fill in the missing words. Then listen and check your answers.

Tom: Would you like to go .... tonight?
a movie   to a movie

Jodi: Tonight? Sure. What's .... ?
play   playing

Tom: *Friday's Child*, with Tom Cruise, is playing ....
the   at the
Festival Cinema.

Jodi: Hmm. That sounds ....
good   well

Tom: OK, let's go ....
see   watch
it. It .... 8:30.
starts   starts at

Jodi: That's perfect.

Now practice the conversation.

2 LISTENING

Listen and write the correct information. Which event do they talk about? When is it? Can they go together?

1. Event: _____
   When: _____
   Can they go together? _____

2. Event: _____
   When: _____
   Can they go together? _____

3 PRONUNCIATION TIP

HOW TO

Say "would"

You need to use your lips, tongue, and breath to pronounce this sound correctly.

Start with /u/

Blow out quickly.

Finish with /ʊ/

Now say the whole word: would.

Listen and repeat. Concentrate on /wʊd/.

1. Would you like to go to a movie tonight?

2. Would you like to go out for dinner tomorrow?

3. Would you like to go dancing on Friday night?

4. Would you like to see a football game this weekend?

5. Would you like to take a trip this summer?

4 PRACTICE

Look at the pictures. Take turns. Choose an activity and a time. Invite your partner. Your partner will answer.

EXAMPLE

Would you like to go out for dinner?
  Sure. I'd love to. When?
How about Friday evening?
  Sorry, I can't.
  How about on Saturday?
That sounds good.

- on Friday evening
- the day after tomorrow
- tomorrow
- this weekend
- tonight
- right now

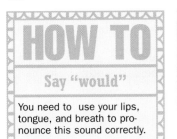
❶ hang out together

❷ sing karaoke

❸ do something together

❹ go out for a drink

❺ take a trip to (place)

❻ go for a drive

❼ see a football game

❽ go out for dinner

❾ go dancing

5 EXCHANGE

Think of two activities to do this weekend.

_____   _____

Stand up. Talk to your classmates.
Invite each person to one activity. Accept some invitations and turn down some invitations.

CULTURE TIP

Give a reason.
"I'm afraid I can't. I have to study."

BASIC CONVERSATION

Would you like to go dancing this weekend?
Sure. When?
How about Saturday night?
That sounds great.

BONUS

Try to use some of these expressions.

ACCEPTING (SAYING YES)
•That sounds nice.

NOT SURE
•Maybe. I don't know right now.

DECLINING (SAYING NO)
•No, sorry, I can't.
•Sorry. Maybe some other time.

REASONS
•I already have plans.
•I should stay home and study.

6 VOCABULARY BUILDING

Put these "frequency expressions" in the correct row.

once a week   every now and then   not very often   occasionally
a lot   once in a while   rarely   almost never
almost every day   as often as I can   once in a blue moon hardly ever

seldom	
sometimes	
often	

Now say three sentences about yourself using these expressions.

7 SMALL TALK: POPULAR ACTIVITIES

Every few years a new kind of entertainment becomes popular.

- In the 1950s bowling became very popular.
- In the 1960s drive-in movies started to become popular.
- In the 1970s there was disco.
- In the 1980s karaoke started to spread around the world.
- In the 1990s computer networking became a popular form of entertainment.

Talk about these questions with your classmates.

What is a popular kind of entertainment now?

What is a kind of entertainment activity that is popular only in your country?

8 COMMUNICATION TASK *Places to try*

Think of some places to tell your partner about:

.... ┐
....
....
....
.... ├ is a good place to ┬ sing karaoke.
.... │ listen to live music.
.... │ work out.
.... │ hang out with friends.
.... │ go dancing.
.... │ go jogging.
.... ┘ relax.
                         see interesting people.
                         go out for dinner.
                         meet people.

Work with a partner. Ask your partner's opinion about four entertainment activities:

> **EXAMPLE**
>
> What is a good place to sing karaoke?
> *I like the Red Lion. There are always a lot of people there.*

COMMUNICATION

GOAL

*What new places
did you learn about?*

•

9 GRAMMAR CHECK

Choose the correct words to complete the story.

I .... (live / have lived) in San Francisco for one year. When I .... (move / moved) here, I was very

.... (bored / boring) because I had no .... (friend / friends). Now I have a lot of friends and

.... (go out / going out) a lot on the weekends. There are many .... (stuff / things) to do here.

Last Friday I went to a .... (dance / danced) club and learned how to dance the "salsa."

It was a lot of .... (fun / funny). Most .... (week / day) nights I .... (meet / am meeting) some friends at a

local coffee shop. I enjoy .... (to talk / talking) with them. Now I love San Francisco because I am

.... (always / never) lonely.

ACTIVITY 1 SPEAKING CIRCLES

VERB TENSES	GRAMMAR TARGETS	
Present Progressive	What **are** you do**ing**?	I **am** (I'**m**) watch**ing** television.
	What **is** she read**ing**?	She **is** (She'**s**) read**ing** the newspaper.
	Who **is** Tom talk**ing** to?	He **is** (He'**s**) talk**ing** to Barbara.
Present Perfect (1)	**Have** you ever **been** to Sam's Jazz Club?	Yes, I **have**. / No, I **haven't**.
	Have you ever **tried** sky-diving?	Yes, I **have**. I **tried** it six years ago. No, I **haven't**. I'**ve never tried** it.
	Have you ever **eaten** sushi?	Yes, I **have**. I'**ve eaten** it many times.

❶ Sit in two rows. Face each other.
❷ Start with TOPIC 1.
❸ Talk to your partner for 1 minute.
❹ Then change partners.
❺ Talk for 1 minute about the same topic.
❻ Continue for 3 or 4 partners.
❼ Start again on TOPIC 2 with a new partner.

TOPIC 1 — PERSONAL DESCRIPTION

Sample questions:
Which people do you know in this class?
How long have you known them?
Who are you talking about?
Do you mean the man sitting in the corner?

TOPIC 2 — FAMILIES

Sample questions:
What's your father like?
Are you living with your parents now?
Have you moved out of your parents' house?
Do you spend a lot of time with your folks?

TOPIC 3 — PLACES AROUND TOWN

Sample questions:
Where's a good coffee shop?
Could you please tell me a good place to buy magazines?
Is there a nice restaurant around here?

CULTURE TIP

Help your partner express his or her ideas. Ask questions.

TOPIC 4 — ENTERTAINMENT

Sample questions:
What is a good place to hear some rock and roll music?
Would you like to go out for coffee sometime next week?
How about going to breakfast on Thursday morning?

ACTIVITY 2 ROLE PLAY

**Work with a partner. Choose a situation. Make up a dialogue.
Practice your dialogue. Then say your dialogue in front of the class.**

EXAMPLE

A couple are deciding what to do.

Andrea: What do you want to do tonight?
Lance: *Let's go out and listen to some music.*
Andrea: OK. That sounds good. Any ideas?
Lance: *Yeah. I think Pete Marley is playing at...*

SITUATION 1

**Two friends see a well-known actress in
a crowded Hollywood restaurant.**

Possible Expressions:

Which woman is the movie star?

I'm going to go over and ask for
her autograph!

The woman wearing the white dress?

Are you sure it's her?

SITUATION 2

**A tourist needs help finding
some places.**

Possible Expressions:

Are you looking for something?

Help! I need to find my hotel.

How long will it take to get there?

Do you want me to take you there?

COMMUNICATION
TIP

Listen to your partner
carefully before you respond.

SITUATION 3

**A young woman and her American
boyfriend discuss their families.**

Possible Expressions:

Are you thinking of introducing me to
your parents?

My family eats dinner together every
Wednesday.

My sister saw your picture and said you
were handsome.

When can I meet them?

SITUATION 4

A couple are deciding what to do on the weekend.

Possible Expressions:

Let's go to the beach on Sunday.

Are we staying home today?

Why don't we rent videos on Saturday?

Why don't we try something new?

14 Personal Items

GRAMMAR TARGETS

Looking for Something	What	are	you they	looking for?	I'm They're She's He's	looking for	my their her his	suitcase.
		is	she he	trying to find?		trying to find		

Describing an Object	What **does** it look like?	It's	brown. black. pink.		It's	round. square. S-shaped.
		It **has**	a black case. two large pockets. my name on it.		**It's made of**	leather. plastic. wood.

W A R M U P *Look at one unusual object in the room. Can you describe it*

1 CONVERSATION 📟

Look at the picture. *Where are they? What is happening?*

Fill in the missing words. Then listen and check your answers.

Rick: What _____ for?
          do you look   are you looking

Walt: _____ watch.
          My   Mine

Rick: What _____ like?
          it's look   does it look

Walt: It _____ gold and it
          is   has
_____ a brown leather band.
is   has

Rick: _____ ?
          Is it   Is this it

Walt: Yeah. Thanks a million.

Now practice the conversation.

66

2 LISTENING 📟

Listen and write the correct information. What are they looking for? How do they describe it?

1. She's looking for .... 2. He's looking for ....

Description: .... Description: ....

3 PRONUNCIATION TIP 📟

HOW TO

Connect "What are you...?" and "What does...?"

In conversation, we naturally connect "grammar" words like *does, do, you, it, is, are.* This helps with the rhythm of speaking.

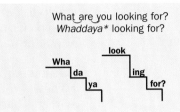

What are you looking for?
*Whaddaya** looking for?

Wha
da
ya
look
ing
for?

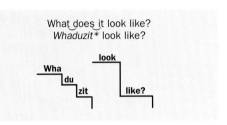

What does it look like?
*Whaduzit** look like?

Wha
du
zit
look
like?

Listen and repeat. Mark the stressed syllables.
Say *"whaddaya"* and *"whaduzit"* quietly and very smoothly.

1. *Whaddaya*
   Whaddaya look
   Whaddaya looking for?

2. *Whaddaya*
   Whaddaya search
   Whaddaya searching for?

3. *Whaduzit*
   Whaduzit look
   Whaduzit look like?

*This is not normal spelling. These forms are not in the dictionary.

4 PRACTICE

Look at the pictures. Choose an item. Describe it to your partner.

EXAMPLE

What are you looking for?
   I'm looking for my wallet.
What does it look like?
   It's black and made of leather.

5 EXCHANGE

**Stand up. Put some items around the room.
Then walk around the room. Ask about your items.**

BASIC CONVERSATION

Excuse me. Can you help me?
I'm looking for my Walkman.
What does it look like?
It's black and has a leather case.
Is that it?

BONUS

Try to use some of these expressions.

ASKING
•Did you lose something?

ASKING FOR HELP
•Can you help me? I've lost something.

HELPING
•Maybe it's over there.
•Could it be in your bag?

EXPRESSING RELIEF
•Whew! I found it.
•Great! That's it.

6 VOCABULARY BUILDING

Work with a partner. Can you think of two items for each column?

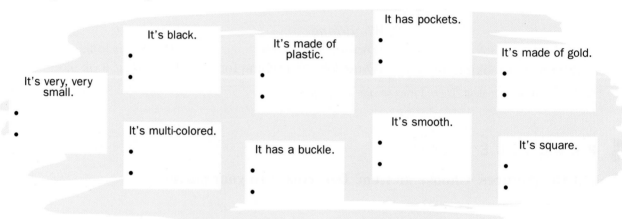

It's black.

It's made of
plastic.

It has pockets.

It's made of gold.

It's very, very
small.

It's multi-colored.

It has a buckle.

It's smooth.

It's square.

Can you say one more thing about each item?

7 SMALL TALK: CLASSIC ITEMS

Some items are classics – they stay around forever. One
classic item is the Swiss Army Knife. There are several
versions of this knife. The most complicated one has 25 different attachments, including nail clippers and a corkscrew.
Originally, the knife was part of the equipment for the
national army of Switzerland. Now the Swiss Army Knife can
be bought in sporting goods stores around the world.

Talk about these questions with your classmates.

SOME ITEMS ARE:
large blade
small blade
corkscrew
can opener with small
screwdriver
bottle opener with large
screwdriver
reamer scissors
phillips screwdriver
magnifying glass
wood saw
metal saw
fish scaler
hook
pliers with wire cutter
chisel
fine screwdriver
ball point pen
straight pin
key ring
tweezers
toothpick

*Do you own any
"classic" items?*

*Do you collect
anything?
(comic books, posters,
boxes, dolls?)*

8 COMMUNICATION TASK  *Special items*

Think of a special item that you have with you or at home.

Work in a group of four. Ask only yes/no questions to find out about your partners' special items.

EXAMPLE

Is it made of gold?
Yes, it is.
Is it larger than my hand?
No, it isn't.

COMMUNICATION
GOAL

Who has the most interesting item?

•

Special Items

9 GRAMMAR CHECK

Fill in the blanks to complete the story. Use some of these words.

cloth	leather	brown	pair	carry	zip	thing
clothes	shoes	plastic	pairs	carrying	zipper	stuff
accessory	shoe	pocket	jean	has	for	cotton
accessories	gold	pockets	jeans	have	from	

Let me tell you about some of my favorite .... and .... My favorite

.... to wear is a loose black .... sweater. I also like to wear an old

.... of black .... Most of the time, I wear my white ....

running .... I usually wear a .... necklace. It was a gift

.... my grandmother. It .... a small heart charm on it. I always

.... a large .... purse with me. It has two big

.... and a large silver ....

15 Cities

UNIT

GRAMMAR TARGETS						
Opinions	I	(really)	**like** **love**	Tokyo. New York.		
	I **don't**	(really)	**like**	Los Angeles. London.		
Comparisons	I think New York **is**		**better** **worse**		**than**	Honolulu.
	In my opinion, Seoul **is**		**more** exciting **less** dangerous		**than**	Shanghai.
Explaining Your Opinion	New York	**has**	**more** interesting places **fewer** music clubs		**than**	Tokyo.
	Seoul		**better** transportation **worse** pollution		**than**	Shanghai.

W A R M   U P   *What is your favorite city? Why?*

1 CONVERSATION 📠

Look at the picture. *Where are they? What is happening?*

Fill in the missing words. Then listen and check your answers.

Lana: You've _____ to a lot of
          be   been
different cities. What do
you _____ New York?
     think   think of

Yuki: I really _____ New York.
              fond of   like

Lana: Yeah, _____, too. I think
                  I   me
it's _____ than Tokyo.
     exciting   more exciting

Yuki: Yes, and the people are
_____ friendly, _____.
  more   most   too   isn't it

Lana: Really? Do you _____ so?
                          say   think

Now practice the conversation.

2 LISTENING 📟

Listen and write the correct information. What cities are they talking about? What do they think?

1. Cities: _____

   Opinion: _____

2. Cities: _____

   Opinion: _____

3 PRONUNCIATION TIP 📟

HOW TO

Use Stress to Make a Comparison

Be sure to use stress and pausing to help the listener understand.

Use stress and pausing.

1. Stress what you want to compare.

2. Pause after the first stress.

3. Change /thæn/ to /thən/. Make it quiet.

■ · ■ · · ■ · · ■ ■ ■ · ■ · ■ ·
New **York** | is more exciting *thən* **Tok**yo.

Listen. Mark the stressed syllables and where to pause.

1. Seoul is less crowded than Shanghai.
2. People are more friendly in Honolulu than in New York.
3. Sondra has more friends in Rio de Janeiro than in Recife.
4. Helen thinks Paris is more interesting than London.

Listen again and repeat.

4 PRACTICE

Look at the pictures. Take turns. Choose two cities. Ask questions. Your partner will give an opinion.

EXAMPLE

Which city would you like to live in, Beijing or Hong Kong?
   I would like to live in Hong Kong.
Why?
   Because I think Hong Kong is more exciting than Beijing.

Opinion Ideas:
is more beautiful, is more peaceful, is more exciting, is less crowded, is less dangerous, has more exciting activities, has more interesting places, has less pollution

Hong Kong, China

❷ Beijing, China

Washington D.C., U.S.A.

❸ New York, U.S.A.

Rome, Italy

❶ Milan, Italy

Oxford, England

❹ London, England

Tokyo, Japan

❺ Kyoto, Japan

5 EXCHANGE

Think of five cities. Talk to your classmates. Ask their opinions about different cities.

CULTURE TIP

Ask for reasons and examples. This will deepen the conversation. **"Why do you think so? Why do you like...? What do you like about it?"**

BASIC CONVERSATION

Which city would you prefer to live in, _____ or _____?

I would prefer to live in _____.

Why?

Because....

BONUS

Try to use some of these expressions.

ASKING
- Would you rather live in ___ or ___?
- Why do you prefer ___ over ___?

ANSWERING
- ___ seems safer than ___.
- ___ is too crowded for me.

GIVING A PREFERENCE
- I'd rather live in _____.
- I don't know. I've never been to ___.

EXPLAINING
- I wouldn't want to live in ___ because it's too cold.

6 VOCABULARY BUILDING

Work with a partner. Make 12 sentences. In each sentence include one item from each box. *Example: In May it's rainy in Portland.*

MONTH			WEATHER			CITY		
January	February	March	cloudy	hot	freezing	Sidney	London	San Francisco
April	May	June	windy	foggy	snowy	Osaka	New Delhi	Montreal
July	August	September	cold	sunny	humid	Prague	Moscow	Lima
October	November	December	warm	stormy		Bogota	Seoul	Beijing

7 SMALL TALK: THE PERFECT CITY

According to *Money* magazine, Madison, Wisconsin, is one of the best cities to live in in the United States. Here are the reasons that people like "Mad Town":

- ideal size, about 400,000 people, so it's not too big or too small
- a lot of new jobs with an unemployment rate of only 1.5%
- wonderful schools for children
- very little crime
- affordable housing
- near a major university (University of Wisconsin)
- 190 sunny days a year.

Talk about these questions with your classmates.

In your country, what is the best city to live in?

What do you like about your city?

Do you like living in a city or in the suburbs?

8 COMMUNICATION TASK *Best cities*

Write the names of 11 different cities in your country.

a beautiful city

a famous city

a city with very friendly people

a polluted city

a dangerous city

an interesting city

an expensive city

a modern city

a small city

a city with bad weather

a city that is too big

COMMUNICATION

GOAL

Which cities do you and your partner agree about?

•

Now work with a partner. Say your opinion about your 11 cities. Does your partner agree or disagree? Compare your ideas.

EXAMPLE

What do you think is a modern city?
I think Osaka is modern.
How about you?

9 GRAMMAR CHECK

Choose the correct words to complete each sentence.

1. I like Dallas because the people are _____ friendly.
   so   too

2. Los Angeles was very _____ in the 1970s, but now it's not so _____ .
   pollution   polluted   good   bad

3. I like _____ in Paris because there _____ so many _____ activities.
   live   living   is   are   excite   exciting

4. Marco has _____ relatives in Rio de Janiero, and he visits _____ often.
   much   many   him   them

5. I'd like to _____ to San Francisco because the _____ is so nice.
   move   moving   weather   seasons

6. London is _____ .
   interest   interesting

7. I'd love to live in Tokyo, but I _____ – it's too _____ .
   can   can't   expense   expensive

8. I _____ to live in Seoul, but now I _____ in Pusan.
   am used   used   live   lives

9. The people _____ Honolulu are more friendly _____ the people in New York.
   of   in   as   than

10. I'd _____ live in Mexico City than in Monterrey _____ there are _____ jobs.
    prefer   rather   so   because   much   more

73

16 Jobs
UNIT

GRAMMAR TARGETS

Asking about Jobs	What	do	you they	do?		I'm They're She's	an actor. teachers. a doctor.
	What	does	she				
Finding Out More	What	do	you they	like dislike	about	your their	job?
	What	does	he she	enjoy hate		his her	
	I They He She		like don't like enjoys hates	visiting talking teaching cooking		clients. to patients. English to beginners. hamburgers.	
Opinions	Your job His job		sounds	interesting. boring			

WARM UP *What is the best job in the world? Why?*

1 CONVERSATION

Look at the picture. *Where are they? What is happening?*

Fill in the missing words. Then listen and check your answers.

April: What do you do ....?
to live   for a living

Jerry: Me? I'm ....
the pilot   a pilot
for British Airlines.

April: Oh, really?

Jerry: Yeah, I mostly ....
fly   am flying
between New York and London.

April: .... interesting.
This is   That's

Jerry: How about you? What .... do?
do you   can you

April: Me? I'm an actor, but .... right now.
I don't work   I'm not working

Now practice the conversation.

2 LISTENING 📻

Listen and write the correct information. What are their jobs? Do they like their jobs?

1. Job: _____

He likes it because _____

2. Job: _____

She doesn't like it because _____

3 PRONUNCIATION TIP 📻

HOW TO

Reduce Grammar Words

If you reduce grammar words, you'll sound more natural.

Full Stressed Form	Reduced Unstressed Form	
do	də	What do you do?
you	yə	
a	ə	I'm a pilot.
for	fər	I'm a pilot for British Airlines.

Full Stressed Form	Reduced Unstressed Form	
to	tə or də	I fly to New York.
and	ən	I fly to New York and London.
an	ən	I'm an actor.

**Listen and repeat. Concentrate on the reduced grammar words.
Say everything in one breath.**

1. *Whaddaya*
   Whaddaya **do**?

2. *I'mə*
   I'mə **pi**lot.

3. *fər* British **Air**lines.
   pilot *fər* British **Air**lines.
   I'mə **pi**lot *fər* British **Air**lines.

4. *flydə*
   flydə New **York**.
   I *flydə* New **York**.

5. *flydə* New **York**
   flydə New **York** *n*
   flydə New **York** *n* **Lon**don.
   I *flydə* New **York** *n* **Lon**don.

6. **nac**
   nactor.
   mə **nac**tor.
   I'mə **nac**tor.

4 PRACTICE

**Look at the pictures. Take turns. Point to a person. Ask questions.
Your partner will answer.**

EXAMPLE

Who's that?
      That's Jack.
What does he do?
      He's an actor.
      Most of the time he reads scripts.
That sounds easy.

❶ Anton and Mark
• machine repairmen
• fix copy machines
• a little boring

❷ Stan and Will
• computer programmers
• make computer games
• cool

❸ Vicki • office manager
• talk on the phone • sort of dull

❹ Valerie • ski instructor
• teach beginner classes • difficult

❺ Jack • actor
• read scripts • easy

❻ Connie • news reporter
• interview people • interesting

❼ Louis • sales manager
• work on his computer • neat

❽ Andrea • sales person
• travel to meet her customers
• exciting

5 EXCHANGE

Think of a job you would like to have:

_____
(or use your real job)

Think about: *What do you like about your job?*
***What do you dislike about your job?* Now stand up.**
Ask your classmates questions about their "job."

BASIC CONVERSATION

What do you do?
   I'm a....
What do you like about your job?
   I like...
What do you dislike about your job?
   I don't like...

BONUS

Try to use some of these expressions.

ASKING FOR AN OPINION
• How do you like it?

TALKING ABOUT YOUR JOB
• Most of the time I work at the office, but sometimes I travel.

EXPRESSING YOUR OPINION
• My job is too stressful.

COMMENTING
• I bet that's interesting.
• Wow, I'm impressed!

6 VOCABULARY BUILDING

Match the expressions in the left column with similar expressions in the right column.

Connie's a news reporter.	He has to fix problems in the programs.
Louis is the sales manager.	He's in a lot of popular movies.
Valerie's a ski instructor.	She takes care of a lot of problems around the office.
Jack is an actor.	He's in charge of sales for the east coast.
Anton is a repairman.	She sells telephone services.
Stan is a computer programmer.	She teaches four or five lessons a day.
Paul is a cook.	He usually fixes copy machines.
Vicki is our office manager.	He works the night shift at Denny's.
Andrea is a sales person.	She's often on the Channel 7 News.
Jerry is a pilot.	He flies between London and New York.

Now think of one more description. Can your partner guess the profession?

7 SMALL TALK: UNUSUAL JOBS

Every profession has some unusual jobs. Have you heard of these jobs?

stunt person
does dangerous "stunts" in movies
(like jumping from a building)
MOVIE INDUSTRY

food stylist
chooses and arranges
food for advertisements
PHOTOGRAPHY INDUSTRY

blaster
blows up buildings
CONSTRUCTION INDUSTRY

chocolatier
tastes new types of chocolate
FOOD INDUSTRY

cruise ship entertainer
performs on stage for
ship passengers
TRAVEL INDUSTRY

Talk about these questions with your classmates.

*What unusual jobs
do you know?*

*What is
the most interesting job
you know?*

8 COMMUNICATION TASK *Dream job*

What is your dream job? Take this questionnaire. Work in a group of four.

	Absolutely	Doesn't matter	Absolutely Not
I like to work outdoors.			
I like to work with people.			
I want to be my own boss.			
I want to make a lot of money.			
I need to have a flexible schedule.			
I want to sit at a desk all day.			
I want to have a lot of stress.			
I want to work at home.			
I want to have an important job.			
I want to do something dangerous.			

Now make two other sentences about your ideal job.

- _____
- _____

Share your answers with your group. Give advice to your partners.

EXAMPLE

The best job for you is _____.
Really? Why do you say that?

COMMUNICATION
GOAL

What jobs did your partners suggest for you?

-

9 GRAMMAR CHECK

Make sentences to match each question or answer.

1. _____ about your job?
   Well, I enjoy helping my students learn.

2. _____?
   I'm in business.

3. Does _____?
   No, he doesn't like the long hours.

4. _____?
   They are biologists.

5. What's _____?
   It's OK. I meet a lot of kind people.

6. Does she enjoy working there?
   No, _____.

7. Does he paint all the time?
   Yes, most _____.

8. What do you two do?
   _____.

9. What do they hate about their jobs?
   _____.

10. Is your job relaxing?
    _____.

Now practice the conversations with a partner.

17 Future Plans

GRAMMAR TARGETS

Asking about Future Actions	What **are**	you they	going to do	this weekend?	
	What **is**	he she			
Answering	I'm We're They're He's She's		going to	work have stay play go	on my project. dinner at Jack's. home. tennis. to Mexico.
Saying a Specific Time	What are you		going to	do	**after** class? **tonight?** **on** Thursday? **in** May? **this** summer? **next** year?

W A R M   U P   *What are you going to do this weekend?*

1 CONVERSATION 📟

Look at the picture. *Where are they? What is happening?*

Fill in the missing words. Then listen and check your answers.

Andy: What _____ do this weekend?
    do you   are you going to

Stacy: I'm going to _____ Las Vegas.
    go   go to

Andy: Las Vegas? What are you going _____ there?
    do   to do

Stacy: I'm going _____ wedding. My boyfriend _____ married _____ Saturday.
    a   to a   will get   is getting   on   in

Andy: Huh?

Now practice the conversation.

78

2 LISTENING 📟

Listen and write the correct information. What are they going to do?

1. Valerie: _____   2. Jack: _____

3 PRONUNCIATION TIP 📟

HOW TO

Reduce "going to" + verb

In conversation, "going to" sounds like "gonna" because it has weak stress.

"going to" + verb

1. Stress the most important word.

2. Say "gonna"/gənə/ for "going to". Make it quiet.

What are you *gənə* **do** this weekend?

*Say "gonna" in normal, natural, relaxed conversation. Write "going to".

Listen. You will hear some sentences with careful pronunciation, then relaxed pronunciation.
Repeat them with relaxed pronunciation. Use *"gonna"*.

4 PRACTICE

Look at the pictures. Take turns. Point to a person.
Ask questions. Your partner will answer.

EXAMPLE

What is Steve going to do next weekend?
He's going to go to the mountains.
To do what?
He's going to go hiking, I guess.

Steve • next weekend
• the mountains • go hiking

Rose • at noon
• the cafe • meet some friends

Carol & Joe • at 3:00 • the shopping mall
• do their Christmas shopping

Sheila • this afternoon
• downtown • walk around

Tim • on Friday night
• a party • enjoy himself

David & Renee • this spring
• the beach • swim

Burt • tomorrow
• his office • finish a report

5 EXCHANGE

**Stand up. Talk to your classmates.
Ask about their plans for:**

- after class today
- tonight
- this weekend
- next year

CULTURE TIP

If you're not sure, give an approximate answer.
"I don't know... I might..."

BASIC CONVERSATION

What are you going to do after class today?
I'm going to meet some friends.
How about tonight?
I'm going to see a movie.

BONUS

Try to use some of these expressions.

NOT SURE
- I may go to see a movie.
- I'm thinking about going to see a movie.

TALKING ABOUT FUTURE ARRANGEMENTS
- I'm getting married on Sunday.
- I'm meeting Jack tonight.

TALKING ABOUT PLANS (DESIRES AND HOPES)
- I'm planning to move to Brazil.
- I hope to be working full-time at IBM.

6 VOCABULARY BUILDING

Put these "future expressions" in the correct row.

someday
after I retire
in a minute
after I graduate

in a few weeks
before I'm 40
tomorrow
next month

next year
after class
in two hours
in a few years

before the end of the year
when I'm an old man (woman)
when this class is over
right now

very near future	
near future	
distant future	

Now say three sentences using these expressions.

7 SMALL TALK: NEW YEAR'S RESOLUTIONS

Every year on New Year's Day, many people make "New Year's Resolutions."
These are promises for the New Year. Here are the most common ones:

- Quit smoking.
- Go jogging every morning.
- Go to the fitness club (twice a week).
- Don't make deadlines I can't keep.
- Pay off my credit card bill.
- Cut down on (alcohol, coffee, junk food).
- Spend more time with my children.
- Find a new job.
- Lose weight.
- Don't forget appointments.
- Read one book (every week).
- Be kind to people.
- Call Mom on her birthday.
- Keep my desk clear.
- Start a new romance.

Talk about these questions with your classmates.

What New Year's resolutions would you like to make?

What future goals do you have?

8 COMMUNICATION TASK — *Plans for the future*

Think about your future. Check your answer for each idea.

I hope to...	Yes, definitely	Yes, probably	No, probably not	No, definitely not	I don't know
learn to speak English well					
live in a foreign country someday					
write an important book					
get married					
become a movie star in the next five years					
be famous someday					
have children					
your idea:					
your idea:					

**Now work in a group of 4. Ask your partners three questions about the future.
Then ask a follow-up question.**

COMMUNICATION GOAL

Which of your partner's ideas surprised you?

•

EXAMPLE

What is something you don't want to do?
I don't want to be famous.
Why not?

9 GRAMMAR CHECK

Work with a partner. Put the words in correct order to make sentences.

1. on are to we do Wednesday going what?

2. some going I'm meet to friends .

3. not might but I I'm Chris sure meet .

4. fly next going they to to month Rome are .

5. may see go I a movie to .

6. graduate to planning at work I after Sony I'm .

7. today what after you are do class to going?

8. have a at to restaurant going breakfast he is .

9. to this planning she's travel spring .

10. to house I have a hope someday nice .

18 Customs

GRAMMAR TARGETS

Advice	I think	you she	should			wear a tie. be on time.
	I think	we he	are is	supposed to		call first. leave early.
	I don't think	you she	should			smoke in here. stay here.
	You're They're	not	supposed to			do that. drink beer.
Wishes	I They	wish	you we	would		stop talking. not push.
Requests	Could you		arrive on time?			
	Would you mind		leaving your dog at home?			

WARM UP *What is an important custom in your country?*

1 CONVERSATION

Look at the picture. *Where are they? What is happening?*

Fill in the missing words. Then listen and check your answers.

Mari: Hi, Mark. Please _____ in.
come   to come

Mark: Thanks, Mari.

Mari: Oh, um, Mark. Would _____
you   it
mind...?

Mark: What?

Mari: Would you mind
_____ your shoes?
take off   taking off

Mark: Oh, sorry. I _____ .
couldn't remember   forgot

Mari: Thanks. We always take off
_____ in the house.
the shoe   our shoes

Now practice the conversation.

2 LISTENING 📼

**Listen and write the correct information. What do they want to do OR
what don't they want to do? What's the rule?**

1. Sam wants to _____ .

    Rule: _____

2. Jason doesn't want to _____ .

    Rule: _____

3 PRONUNCIATION TIP 📼

Connecting words:

dʒ
↑
Would you...? = "Wouldju...?"

dʒ
↑
Could you...? = "Couldju...?"

HOW TO

Connect "Would you...?" and "Could you...?"

Connecting sounds makes you sound more fluent. Sometimes linking two consonants makes a new sound: d + y = j

**Listen. Mark the stressed syllables.
Mark where your voice goes up ‿ . Mark the word connection and
write in the new sound.**

1. Would you mind taking off your shoes?
2. Could you take off your shoes?
3. Would you mind smoking outside?
4. Could you smoke outside?

Listen again and repeat. Say everything in one breath.

4 PRACTICE

**Look at the pictures. Take turns. Choose a picture. Ask your partner what is wrong.
Your partner will answer.**

EXAMPLE

What's wrong?
> *I don't think Arthur should
> touch the paintings.*
You mean he's not supposed to
touch them.
> *Right. It's a rule.*

❸ Colleen
• bring pets into the building

❹ Barbara
• make noise after 10 p.m.

❷ Jane and Greg
• talk in the church

❺ Tony and Sue (kids)
• throw things on the ground

❻ Arthur
• touch the paintings

❼ Carlos and Maria
• speak Spanish in
  English class

ENGLISH-1
John went

❶ Bill and Karen
• let the children play in the aisles

❽ Laura
• take photos in the museum

POP CORN

❾ Kate
• put things on the seats

❿ Herb
• use a tape recorder
  at the concert

5 EXCHANGE

Imagine two new rules for your school.

Examples:
about clothes   about appearance
about time   about class activities

Now stand up. Ask your classmates about their rules.

CULTURE TIP

Don't be shy if you don't understand. Ask for reasons. **"Can you explain that to me?"**

BASIC CONVERSATION

What are your new rules?
    I think we should (shouldn't)....
Yes, that's a good idea.
OR
Hmm, I'm not sure that's a good idea.

BONUS

Try to use some of these expressions.

STATING RULES
- I want people to smoke outside.
- I don't want people to smoke in the building.

ASKING REASONS
- I don't quite understand. Could you explain that to me?
- I don't understand. Why do we need that rule?

GIVING REASONS
- We don't want to disturb other people.
- I think it would be more polite.

6 VOCABULARY BUILDING

Choose a response on the right for each situation on the left.

Situations	Responses
Someone is talking too loudly in the hallway.	"I'm sorry, but I'm afraid you can't use that now."
Someone is bringing a dog into the building.	"Please don't get on that."
Someone spilled something on the floor.	"I think you'd better slow down."
Some children are climbing on the furniture.	"I wish that you wouldn't touch that."
Someone is touching an expensive painting.	"No, thanks. I don't care for any more."
Someone is using a tape recorder at an important meeting.	"Would you wipe that up, please?"
Someone is smoking in your house.	"Would you mind going outside if you need to smoke?"
Your taxi driver is driving too fast.	"Would you mind leaving your pet outside?"
Someone is taking your bag.	"Excuse me. That belongs to me."
The host is serving you more food.	"If you don't mind, could you keep it down?"

Can you think of one more situation?

7 SMALL TALK: SOCIAL CUSTOMS

All cultures have their own social rules. Here are some examples of social rules or customs.

➡ You shouldn't make sounds or talk or laugh while eating.
➡ It's best not to stand too close to someone when talking.
➡ It's important to make a lot of eye contact during a conversation.
➡ You shouldn't smoke around other people who are not smoking.
➡ Always refill someone's glass when it is empty.
➡ Shake hands firmly when you meet someone.
➡ You are expected to drink alcohol when you're at a group party.
➡ Always bring a gift when you visit someone.

Talk about these questions with your classmates.

Which of these are customs in your country?

What are some special customs in your country?

What are some other customs that you know?

8 COMMUNICATION TASK   *Cultural differences*

Work in a group of four. Take turns. Pick a topic. Each person tries to think of a custom in their culture for the topic. Is this custom different in other cultures?

BEING EMBARRASSED

EXAMPLE:
smiling or laughing when you're embarrassed

NAMES

EXAMPLE:
calling someone by his or her first name

HUGGING

EXAMPLE:
hugging someone when you say goodbye

FEET

EXAMPLE:
putting feet on a desk or table

BEING CLOSE

EXAMPLE:
standing close to someone when talking

JOKING

EXAMPLE:
telling jokes at work

GROUPS

EXAMPLE:
forming separate groups at parties

SMOKING

EXAMPLE:
smoking on a train

PARTIES

EXAMPLE:
refilling someone's glass with beer or wine

BEING ON TIME

EXAMPLE:
arriving exactly on time for a dinner appointment

EATING

EXAMPLE:
making sounds while eating

GESTURES

EXAMPLE:
waving to someone

EXAMPLE

Tell me about a custom related to "hugging."
In _____, we always hug when we say good-bye.

COMMUNICATION GOAL

What new customs did you learn?

---

9 GRAMMAR CHECK

Find the grammar error in each sentence and correct it.

1. In Japan you should taking your shoes off when you enter a house.
2. In Italy you can to eat pasta twice a day.
3. In many countries, you shouldn't to point at someone.
4. In France you should try speak French.
5. In Germany you should have shake hands the first time you meet someone.
6. In the U.S. you don't have take your shoes off when entering a house.
7. In Spain it's not polite talk loudly in a restaurant.
8. In England you don't have to drink tea at 4:00. You can to drink coffee, if you like.
9. In China the people usually don't to talk about business during a meal.
10. On American airplanes you can't be smoke.

ACTIVITY 1 SPEAKING CIRCLES

GRAMMAR TARGETS

Present Perfect (2)	How long **have** you work**ed** here?	I **have** (I**'ve**) work**ed** here for five years.
	How many times **have** you **been** to the States?	I**'ve been** there twice.
	How many years **have** you studi**ed** English?	I**'ve** studi**ed** it for many years.
Wishes	Do you have a car?	No, I don't. But I **wish** I **had** one.
	Would you like to live in Europe?	Yes, I **would** (I**'d**) **love** to live there.
	Did you **speak** English when you were a child?	No, I **didn't**, but I **wish** that I **had** (spoken English).

❶ Sit in two rows. Face each other.
❷ Start with TOPIC 1.
❸ Talk to your partner for 1 minute.
❹ Then change partners.
❺ Talk for 1 minute about the same topic.
❻ Continue for 3 or 4 partners.
❼ Start again on TOPIC 2 with a new partner.

CULTURE TIP

Don't worry about making grammar mistakes. Think about the meaning.

TOPIC 1

PERSONAL ITEMS

Sample questions:
What is your favorite item you own?
Have you seen a laptop computer before?
Do you own a lot of things?

TOPIC 2

CITIES

Sample questions:
Have you ever been to a foreign country?
Which cities would you like to live in?
What do you think would be the worst city to live in?

TOPIC 3

JOBS

Sample questions:
Do you have a job right now?
What type of work would you like to do?
Have you ever worked in a large company?

TOPIC 4

FUTURE PLANS

Sample questions:
What are you planning to do this weekend?
What are you going to do after you learn English?
Have you made plans to travel this year?

TOPIC 5

CUSTOMS

Sample questions:
Have you been surprised by a custom in a foreign country?
Do you think this country has any strange customs?
Which country do you think has the strangest customs?
Are there any rules that you would make for this class?

ACTIVITY 2 ROLE PLAY

Work with a partner. Choose a situation. Make up a dialogue.
Practice your dialogue. Then say your dialogue in front of the class.

EXAMPLE

Susan: What's wrong?
Allen: *I've lost my contact lens.*
Susan: Oh, no! Where did you lose it?
Allen: *Right here. Near the steps.*

CULTURE
TIP

Cooperate with your partner.
"What do you think...?"

SITUATION 1

Two people are looking for an earring in a movie theater.

Possible Expressions:

What are you looking for?

Is your earring gold or silver?

Maybe you should check at the lost and found.

I should wait until the lights are turned on.

SITUATION 2

A couple are thinking about moving to New York City.

Possible Expressions:

Which city has the lowest cost of living?

Have you ever been to New York?

Maybe we should go for a visit there first.

I think that our city is safer than New York.

SITUATION 3

Two strangers are talking during a long plane flight.

Possible Expressions:

What do you do?

That sounds interesting. Do you like it?

I am unemployed at the moment, but I am an actor.

Why did you decide to do that kind of work?

SITUATION 4

Someone visits a fortune teller to ask about the future.

Possible Expressions:

Where am I going to be next year?

Will I be happy in the future?

What's going to happen to me?

You're going to be very...

SITUATION 5

A tour guide discusses some local customs with a tourist.

Possible Expressions:

Should I bring a gift when I visit someone's house?

In my country some people hug when they say hello.

You aren't supposed to pay for the meal.

Am I supposed to tip the waitress?

APPENDIX: TAPE SCRIPTS

UNIT 1 LISTENING

1. A: Hi.
   B: Hi.
   A: How do you like this class?
   B: Oh, it's OK. I like it.
   A: Yeah, me, too. Oh, I'm Linda Barton.
   B: I'm Mike Adams.
   A: It's nice to meet you.

2. A: Hello – you're Susan Martin, right?
   B: Yes, and you're...?
   A: I'm Alex Brown.
   B: Glad to meet you, Mr. Brown.
   A: Oh, you...you can call me Alex. How's your first day on the job?
   B: Fantastic. I like working here.

UNIT 2 LISTENING

1. A: Wow, this is sweet. What is it called?
   B: You don't know? It's called apple pie.
   A: Apple pie?
   B: Yes, it's an American dessert. It's really popular in the States.

2. A: I forgot. What are these called?
   B: Those? They're Danish rolls.
   A: Of course, Danish rolls. So they come from Denmark?
   B: Yes, I guess they're a kind of Danish pastry.

UNIT 3 LISTENING

1. A: Sue, I'll meet you at your office. What's your address?
   B: 221 Market Street.
   A: 220 Market. Great. See you soon.
   B: Wait! I said 221 Market, not 220.
   A: 221? OK, I got it now. I'll be there in a few minutes.

2. A: Can you fax that report to me tonight?
   B: OK, sure.
   A: My fax number is 432-2343.
   B: Did you say 432-3234?
   A: No, 432-2343.
   B: OK, I'll send it around 8:00.

UNIT 4 LISTENING

1. A: I like your shoes. They're very stylish.
   B: Thanks.
   A: Where did you get them?
   B: I bought them last summer in Rome.
   A: Mm.

2. A: That sweater looks wonderful on you.
   B: Thanks. It's new.
   A: It looks really soft. Where did you get it?
   B: It was a present. My husband gave it to me for Christmas.

UNIT 5 LISTENING

1. A: Hey, Molly, are you interested in music?
   B: Sure, I like most kinds of music.
   A: Do you have a favorite kind?
   B: Sure, country. I just love country music.

2. A: What do you guys like to do in your free time?
   B: Oh, we like to hang out in the park.
   C: Yeah, we really like to go Roller-blading at Golden Gate Park.
   B: Yeah, we usually go on Sundays, and sometimes after dinner during the week.

UNIT 6 LISTENING

1. A: I need to get some coffee. Let's stop at Cafe Mocha. They have the freshest coffee beans.
   B: Really? I bet it's super expensive.
   A: Yeah, it is a little expensive.
   B: How much is, say, a small bag of good coffee?
   A: I think it's about 15 dollars now.
   B: 15 dollars!? Are you kidding?

2. A: Honey, let's get a bottle of champagne.
   B: Champagne?
   A: Yeah, it's our anniversary. Come on. Let's celebrate.
   B: OK. Let's do it.
   A: Here's a bottle of good French champagne.
   B: Wow. That's a hundred dollars!
   A: Oh, come on, Max, don't worry about money tonight!

UNIT 7 LISTENING

1. A: Hey, Brad, what did you do last weekend?
   B: I drove up to Boston.
   A: Boston? Your parents live there, right?
   B: Right.
   A: Did you visit them?
   B: Yeah, it was my parents' 25th anniversary. Big party. Lots of people. It was great.

2. A: Hi, guys. How was your weekend?
   B: It was fun, but too short.
   A: What did you do on Sunday? It was such a beautiful day.
   C: We had a picnic in the park with some of my friends from work.
   A: Sounds nice.

UNIT 8 LISTENING

1. A: I heard that Karen moved into a new place. What's her new apartment like?
   B: It's a great place. It's really bright. It's got these big windows in the living room.
   A: Oh, Karen must love that.
   B: Yeah, she has lots of plants. It's like a garden in there!

2. A: Did you stop by at Marco's house?
   B: Yeah. His room is really... um...
   A: Messy, right?
   B: Yeah, he's got all this computer and stereo equipment everywhere... it's so crowded.
   A: But he likes it that way.
   B: Yeah, I guess so.

UNIT 9 LISTENING

1. A: Hi, Kyle, this is JoAnn.
   B: Hi, JoAnn. How are you?
   A: Fine. Kyle, the reason I called is I'm trying to find someone to babysit this weekend.
   A: Babysit? You mean babysit for Carla and Tommy?
   B: Yeah. Can you?
   A: Oh, gosh, JoAnn. I'm sorry. I can't babysit. I'm terrible with kids.

2. A: Listen, Laura. My car is making this strange sound. Can you hear that?
   B: Mm. Yeah, it's your fan belt.
   A: My fan belt?
   B: Yeah, it's loose. I can fix that for you.
   A: Really? You can?
   B: Sure. I work on cars all the time.

Pronunciation Tip:
1. I can sing. 2. I can't draw. 3. She can't do aerobics.
4. He can play baseball. 5. They can't play the piano.

UNIT 10 LISTENING

1. A: I've never met your mother, Lyn. What's she like?
   B: My mom's a lot of fun.
   A: Really?
   B: She is more like my friend than my mom.
   A: How so?
   B: Like we go shopping together on the weekends, and sometimes we go to concerts or movies together.
   A: Oh, she sounds cool.

2. A: What's your dad like?
   B: My dad's OK. He's a bit strange, though.
   A: What do you mean, "strange"?
   B: Well, not strange. Just a little unusual. He's a homemaker.
   A: A what?
   B: A homemaker. He stays home and takes care of the house and kids. My mom goes out to work every day.
   A: Oh.

UNIT 11 LISTENING

1. A: Excuse me, sir?
   B: Yes, can I help you?
   A: Yes, I'm a little lost. Where is the University Hospital?
   B: The hospital? It's on the corner of Third Avenue and Main Street.
   A: Third Avenue and Main?
   B: Yes, just walk down Main. You'll see it on the left side.

2. A: Hey, Judy, we're almost out of gas. Is there a gas station near here?
   B: Hmm. The closest gas station is at Center Street.
   A: Center Street?
   B: Yeah, just go straight. It's about 4 or 5 more blocks.

UNIT 12 LISTENING

1. A: Who's that handsome man talking with Gloria?
   B: Do you mean the short man wearing the glasses?
   A: No, no, not him. I mean the tall man with the beard.
   B: Oh, that's her husband, Jay. Yes, he is handsome.

2. A: That woman standing in the corner is really attractive. Who is she?
   B: Which woman?
   A: Over there, by the door.
   B: Oh, the woman wearing the purple scarf?
   A: Are you blind? The thin woman with the red hat on.
   B: Oh, that one. That's Martha Swan.

UNIT 13 LISTENING

1. A: I'm bored.
   B: Would you like to go to the Giants game tonight?
   A: A baseball game? Sure. Can we still get tickets?
   B: Yeah, no problem. The game starts at 6:00.
   A: All right.
   B: Then we'd better get ready.

2. A: Hello?
   B: Hi, Bob. This is Jane.
   A: Hi, Jane. What's up?
   B: Would you like to play tennis tomorrow?
   A: Tomorrow? What time?
   B: I've got a court from 10 to noon.
   A: Sorry, I can't. I have to work tomorrow morning.

UNIT 14 LISTENING

1. A: Yikes! I lost my wedding ring.
   B: Don't panic. What does it look like?
   A: It's gold and has a small diamond.
   B: You mean this ring on the sink?
   A: Oh, thanks! I forgot I put it there.

2. A: What are you looking for?
   B: I'm trying to find my sunglasses.
   A: Do they have blue glass and gold wire frames?
   B: Yeah, how did you know?
   A: They're on top of your head!

UNIT 15 LISTENING

1. A: I really want to leave New York and move to San Francisco.
   B: Really, Mark? I thought you liked New York.
   A: Yeah, but I just hate the winters here. The weather in San Francisco is much better.
   B: Well, yeah, you're right about that.

2. A: Joan, would you rather visit Hong Kong or Singapore?
   B: Hmm. I'd want to visit Hong Kong, I guess.
   A: Why?
   B: Shopping. There are more places to shop in Hong Kong.

UNIT 16 LISTENING

1. A: What do you do?
   B: I serve drinks at the Hard Rock Cafe.
   A: Oh, that's right. You're a bartender. That sounds like a hard job.
   B: No, it's usually pretty simple. I like it because I get to meet a lot of different people.

2. A: So enough about me. What kind of work do you do?
   B: I'm a receptionist at State Farm Insurance.
   A: A receptionist? Do you like answering the phone all day?
   B: No, it's pretty boring. I do the same thing all day long.

UNIT 17 LISTENING

1. A: What are you going to do this weekend?
   B: This weekend is the beginning of my vacation. I'll be driving across the country.
   A: Really? To Vancouver?
   B: Yeah.
   A: Will you be there by Sunday?
   B: No, by Sunday, I'll be somewhere in Alberta.

2. A: I finally finished that marketing project.
   B: Oh, congratulations. You ought to take a break.
   A: I'm going to. I'm going to take a few days off and go camping.
   B: Oh? Where are you going to go?
   A: I'm not going to tell you... I'm not going to tell anybody.
   B: OK. Well, have a good time!

Pronunciation Tip
1. What are you going to do this weekend? 2. I'm going to go to Las Vegas. 3. What are you going to do

tonight? 4. I'm going to stay at home. 5. What's Shelly going to do after class today? 6. She's going to buy some food. 7. What are Dave and Cathy going to do tomorrow? 8. They're going to meet some friends.

UNIT 18 LISTENING

1. A: Gosh, I really need to have a cigarette. Do you know if I can smoke on this plane?
   B: I'm not sure. Maybe you should ask the flight attendant.
   A: Excuse me, is it OK if I smoke?
   C: I'm sorry, sir. This is a non-smoking flight.

2. A: Jason, I wish you would wear a tie.
   B: Why?
   A: We're going to a fancy club. I think men who go there are supposed to wear ties.
   B: I don't want to put a tie on.
   A: Could you please just wear a tie? I don't want to get into a fight right now.
   B: Fine!

Basics in Speaking uses a 1000 key word vocabulary

The number after the word shows the unit in which the word or expression first appears.
The numbers 1-18 refer to the Main Units; F1-4, F5-9, F10-13, F14-18 refer to the Fluency Units.

200 VERBS

accept, 4
agree, 9
allow, 9
answer, 1
argue, 10
arrive, 18
ask, 3
avoid, 18
babysit, 7
be, 1
be born, 7
be in charge of, 17
be made of, 14
be out of, 11
be worth, 6
beat, 9
become, 17
begin, F1-4
believe, 6
bet, 5
break, 7
bring, 10
build, 9
burn, 18
buy, 4
call, 1
carry, 6
catch, 9
celebrate, 6
change, 10
check, 13
choose, 16
clean, 7
climb, 9
collect, 10
come from, 2
come, 6
compare, 15
complain, 10
complete, 13
cook, F1-4
cost, 6
dance, 9
date, 1
decide, F5-9
decorate, F5-9
describe, 10
dislike, 16
disturb, 18
do, 2
draw, 8
drive, 7
eat, 7
enjoy, 10
explain, 18
export, 2
fall down, 9
fax, 3
fight, 17
fill, 1
find, 11
finish, 17
fix, 9
fly, 16
fool, 7
fond of, 15

forget, 2
form, 18
get, 4
get along with, 10
get angry, 10
get married, 17
give, 4
go, F1-4
go camping, 5
go hiking, 5
go jogging, 5
go out, 1
go shopping, 6
go skiing, 5
graduate, 7
grow up, 9
guess, 2
hang, 12
hang around, 13
hang out, 5
happen, 1
hate, 10
have, 3
have a date, 7
have a hard time, 9
have children, 17
have fun, 7
have trouble, F5-9
hear, 7
help, F1-4
hold, 12
hope, 17
hug, 18
identify, 3
imagine, 4
include, 8
interested in, 1
interview, 17
introduce, F10-13
invite, 8
join, 5
jump, 16
keep, 9
kid, 6
kiss, 9
know, 2
label, 3
laugh, 10
learn, 3
let, 6
lift, 9
like, 1
listen, 5
live, 3
look, 4
look for, 11
love, 5
make, 7
match, 2
mean, 9
meet, 1
mind, 3
move, 8
need, 6
open, 2
pack, 8
paint, 5
panic, 14

pardon, 3
plan, 17
play, 5
point, 1
practice, 1
prefer, 15
produce, 6
push, 18
put, 14
read, 3
refill, 18
register, F1-4
remember, 1
rent, F10-13
repeat, 3
ride, 9
Roller blade, 9
roller skate, 9
save, 6
say, 3
see, 1
sell, 6
send, 3
separate, 18
shake, 18
share, 5
sing, 5
sit, F1-4
skate, 9
sleep, 8
slow down, 18
smile, 18
smoke, 18
snowboard, 9
speak, 9
spend, 6
spill, 18
spread, 13
stand, 9
start, F1-4
stay, 7
stay up, 10
stop, 8
study, 6
suggest, 16
surf, 5
surprise, 7
swim, 9
switch, 3
take, 6
take care, 16
take off, 18
talk, 3
teach, 9
tell, 3
thank, 3
think, 2
tip, F14-18
touch, 18
try, 2
turn, 11
turn down, 13
turn on, F14-18
understand, 9
use, 5
visit, 7
wait, 3
walk, 17

want, F1-4
wash, 7
watch, 5
wave, 18
wear, 4
win, 9
wipe, 18
wish, 18
work, 1
work out, 13
worry, 6
write, 17

200 ADJECTIVES

a bunch of, 9
a few, 3
a little, 1
a lot of, 4
active, 10
adventurous, 10
afraid, 11
American, 2
angry, 10
annoying, 10
athletic, 9
attractive, 12
awful, 4
bad, 2
bald, 12
beautiful, 5
beginning, 17
best, 6
better, 15
big, 7
black, 12
blind, 12
blonde, 12
blue, F1-4
bored, 13
boring, F5-9
both, 9
bright, 8
brown, 14
bushy, 12
casual, 4
challenging, 9
cheap, 6
Chinese, 2
classic, 14
clean, 12
close, 11
cloudy, 15
clumsy, 9
cluttered, 8
cold, 4
comfortable, 8
cool, 4
correct, 1
cotton, 14
cozy, 8
crazy, 10
creative, 9
crowded, 8
curly, 12
dangerous, 10
dark, 12

delicious, 2
different, 9
difficult, 5
distant, 17
dull, 10
dyed, 12
easy, 5
easy-going, 10
embarrassed, 9
enthusiastic, 6
every, 6
excellent, 9
exciting, 5
expensive, 6
extra, 17
fabulous, F1-4
family, 10
famous, 6
fantastic, 1
favorite, 4
female, 12
few, 17
fewer, 15
fine, 6
first, 1
flat, 8
flexible, 16
foggy, 15
foreign, F14-18
freezing, 15
French, 9
fresh, 6
friendly, 15
fulltime, F14-18
funny, 10
glad, 2
gold, 14
good, 2
gorgeous, 6
gray, 12
great, 3
green, 12
handsome, 12
happy, 10
hard, F5-9
Hawaiian, 2
hot, 15
humid, 15
Indian, 12
important, 3
impossible, 9
impressed, 16
international, 2
interested, 1
interesting, 4
Italian, 2
Japanese, 2
jealous, 7
junky, 9
Korean, 2
large, 8
last, 3
lazy, 9
lead, 9
little, 17
lively, 8
local, 13
lonely, 13
long, 12
loose, 9
lost, 4
loud, 8
lovely, 4
low, F14-18
lucky, 3
luxurious, 8
male, 12
married, 7
mean, 10

medium, 12
messy, 8
modern, 1
multi-colored, 14
musical, 9
narrow, 12
natural, 12
neat, 4
nervous, F5-9
new, 2
next, 17
nice, 1
noisy, 8
OK, 3
old, 5
old-fashioned, 8
outgoing, 10
overweight, 12
perfect, 6
personal, F1-4
pink, 14
plastic, 12
pleasant, 12
polluted, 15
popular, 2
possible, 9
pretty, 7
purple, 12
quiet, 8
rainy, 4
ready, 13
red, 12
relaxing, 7
rich, 15
right, 2
round, 14
s-shaped, 14
same, 1
second, 2
serious, 10
short, 12
shy, 9
silver, 14
similar, 10
simple, 11
skinny, 12
small, 8
smart, 16
smooth, 14
snobby, 8
snowy, 15
soft, 4
sorry, 6
Spanish, 18
special, 5
sporty, 4
square, 14
stormy, 15
straight, 11
strange, 8
stressful, 16
strict, 10
strong, 9
stubborn, 10
stylish, 14
sunny, 4
super, F5-9
sweet, 2
tall, 2
terrible, 2
Thai, F5-9
thick, 12
thin, 12
thoughtful, 2
tired, 7
trendy, 4
typical, 7
ugly, 4
uncomfortable, 9

uncrowded, 15
unemployed, F14-18
unusual, 4
warm, 15
wavy, 12
weak, 9
weird, 4
well-known, F10-13
white, F10-13
wide, 12
wild, 4
windy, 15
wonderful, 4
worse, 15
worst, 16
wrong, 3
yellow, 14

50 ADVERB EXPRESSIONS

a bit, 8
a little, 6
absolutely, 16
absolutely not, 16
actually, 3
again, 3
ago, 7
all the time, 10
almost, 11
almost every day, 13
almost never, 13
already, 13
always, 9
at the moment, F14-18
besides, F5-9
completely, 12
definitely, 17
definitely not, 17
easily, 9
early, 18
especially, 5
every day, 10
every now and then, 13
fast, F5-9
fluently, 9
friendly, 15
hopefully, 17
in a minute, 17
just a minute ago, 7
last, 6
late, 10
later, 1
maybe, 2
never, 9
often, 13
occasionally, 13
of course, 2
often, 6
on time, 18
once a week, 13
once in a while, 13
only, 6
outdoors, 10
pretty, 7
probably, 17
probably not, 17
quite, 8
rarely, 13
rather, 3
really, 4
seldom, 13
so, 2
so much, 6
some other time, 13
someday, 17
sometime, 5
sometimes, 8
straight, 11

super, 6
today, 4
together, 1
tomorrow, 13
tonight, 3
too, 2
twice, 18
unique, 8
usually, F1-4
well, 9
yesterday, 4

600 NOUNS

ability, 9
accessories, 4
acquaintance, F5-9
activity, 13
actor, 9
actress, F10-13
address, 3
advice, 10
aerobics, 5
afternoon, 17
airplane, 18
airport, 11
aisle, 18
alarm clock, 6
anniversary, 6
anything, F5-9
anywhere, 10
apartment, 7
apartment number, 3
appearance, 12
apple pie, 2
appointment, 18
April, 15
areas, 6
art, 5
August, 15
aunt, 10
autograph, F10-13
automobile, 6
baby, 15
back, 8
bag, 6
baguette, 2
bakery, 2
balance, 9
ball, 9
balloon, 6
band, 14
bank, 11
bar, 7
bartender, 16
baseball, 2
basketball, 5
beach, 7
beard, 12
bed, 8
beer, 18
beginner, 16
beret, 2
best friends, F1-4
between, 8
bicycle, 9
biologist, 16
bird watching, 5
birth certificate, 3
birthday, 7
birthday present, 6
bistro, F10-13
block, 11
blocks, 9
blue moon, 13
board game, 2
bones, 16
book, 12
boss, 1

bottle, 6
box, 6
boyfriend, 1
bracelet, 4
bread, 2
break, 17
breakfast, F10-13
brother, 1
buckle, 14
building, 18
bus station, 11
bus stop, 11
business, F5-9
business number, 3
business partner, 10
cafe, 17
camera, 6
camping, 5
Canada, 2
candy, 6
car, 5
card, 3
care, 10
cat, 8
CD, 5
cents, 6
championship, 9
charm, 14
chess, 9
child, 9
children, 1
chocolate, 6
Christmas, 6
church, 11
cigarette, 18
cinema, 13
city, 3
class, 1
classmate, 1
clerk, F5-9
cloth, 14
clothes, F1-4
clothing, 2
club, 13
co-worker, 1
coat, 4
coffee, 6
coffee beans, 6
coffee house, 11
coffee shop, 11
coffee, 12
collar, 4
college, F5-9
color, 4
comics, 5
company, 3
compliment, 4
computer, 5
computer game, 5
computer programmer, 16
concert, 17
condo, 8
congratulations, 17
contact lens, 12
convenience store, 11
cook, F1-4
cooking, 5
cookies, 6
copy machine, 16
corner, 11
cosmetics, 6
cost of living, F14-18
cotton, 14
couch, 8
country, 1
country music, 5
couple, F5-9
court, 13
cousin, 10

credit card, F5-9
criminal, 16
culture, 18
custom, 18
customer, F1-4
customs, F14-18
dad, 4
dance music, 2
darts, 5
date, 7
dates, 3
day, 7
December, 15
decorations, 8
dentist, 13
department store, 4
department, 3
description, 14
dessert, 2
dialogue, F1-4
diamond, 14
dinner, F1-4
directions, 16
disagree, 15
DISCman®, 6
disguise, 12
district, 3
divorce, 18
doctor, 1
dog, 1
dollar, 6
donuts, 2
door, 6
downtown, 8
dress, 2
drink, 2
driver's license, 3
driving, 5
drug store, 11
duplex, 8
e-mail address, 3
ear, 4
earring, 6
English, 1
entertainment, 13
entrance exam, 9
equipment, 8
eraser, 6
errands, 7
everybody, 9
everyone, 10
everywhere, 8
exam, 7
excuse, 3
expression F1-4
eyebrows, 12
face, 14
facial hair, 12
fads, 4
falling down, 9
false, 12
family, 10
family name, 3
fan belt, 9
fashion, 4
fast food, 6
father, 7
favor, 14
fax number, 3
February, 15
feet, 4
fiance, 12
fight, 90
fire, 12
first name, 3
fitness, 5
flat, 8
flight, F14-18
flight attendant, 18

floor, 6
folks, F10-13
food, 2
football, 5
fork, 18
form, 3
frames, 14
free time, 5
Friday, 7
friend, 1
fruit, 2
fun, F1-4
furniture, 8
future, 17
gambling, 5
game, 7
garden, 5
gardening, 5
gas, 11
gas station, 11
gift, 4
gift shop, 4
girl, F10-13
girlfriend, 1
glasses, 12
gloves, 4
goal, 17
gold, 14
graduate, 7
graduation, 10
grandfather, 10
grandmother, 10
grandparents, 10
graphic arts, 5
grocery store, 11
ground, 18
guitar, 9
guy, 5
gym, 11
hair, 12
hair band, 12
hair salon, 11
hair style, 12
haircut, F1-4,
hamburger, F5-9
hand, 4
hat, 6
head, 14
heart, 14
heights, 9
high school, 7
hiking, 5
hills, 9
history, 1
hobbies, 10
holiday, 6
home, 7
homemaker, 10
hospital, 11
hotel, 4
hour, 7
house, 8
husband, 4
ice skating, 9
idea, F5-9
identification, 3
information, F1-4
initials, 9
institution, 3
instructor, 16
instrument, 9
insurance, 16
interests, 1
interest group, 5
international, 2
Internet, 5
invitation, 13
item, 2
jacket, 4

January, 15
jazz, 2
jeans, 4
job, 1
jogging, 5
joke, 9
judo, 2
July, 15
June, 15
junk, 8
karaoke, 5
karaoke bar, 9
kids, 9
kilogram, 9
kimchi, 2
kimono, 2
kind, 5
kinds of, F1-4
knee, 9
language, 5
laptop computer, F14-18
last name, 3
league, 9
leather, 14
leg, 4
lesson, 9
library, 7
lights, F14-18
liquor, 2
living room, 8
location, 8
macaroni, 2
magazines, F10-13
magic trick, 9
make-up, 12
man, 12
many, 13
March, 15
martial arts, 2
May, 15
meal, F14-18
meeting, F5-9
member, 5
mile, 11
mind, 10
mini-skirt, 4
minute, 3
modern rock, 5
mom, 7
Monday, 7
money, 6
month, 6
morning, 13
mother, 4
motorcycle, 6
mountain, 9
movie, 5
movie star, F10-13
movie theater, F14-18
museum, 18
music, 5
music club, 15
music store, 11
mustache, 12
name, 1
nan, 2
neat, 4
neck, 4
necklace, 4
neighbor, 1
neighborhood, 8
never, 10
New Year's, 17
news reporter, 16
newspaper, F10-13
niece, 7
night, 7
noon, 13
nose, 12

nothing, 5
November, 15
number, 3
object, 14
October, 15
office, 3
office manager, 16
office phone number, 3
officer, 3
one way street, 3
opera, 2
opinion, 4
outfit, F1-4
pack, 8
pair, 6
panic, 14
parents, 1
park, 5
part, 3
party, F1-4
pasta, 2
Pasta Nora, F1-4
patients, 16
people, F1-4
pet, 5
phone, 3
phone number, 3
photograph, 5
piano, 8
picnic, 7
picture, 5
pie, 2
pilot, 16
place, F1-4
plane, 18
plant, 8
play, 9
pleasant, 12
pocket, 14
poker, 9
politics, 5
pollution, 15
polo, 2
pool, 5
post office, 11
present, 4
price, 6
problem, 9
product, 6
profession, 16
project, 17
pub, 5
purse, 4
question, 3
race track, 5
raincoat, 4
reason, 9
receptionist, 16
record, 9
repairman, 16
restaurant, 2
ring, 14
rock and roll, F10-13
rock music, 1
roll, 2
Rollerblading, 5
Roller-skate, 9
room, 8
roommate, F5-9
rose, 15
rule, 10
safe, 15
sales manager, 16
sales person, 16
salsa, 2
samba, 2
sari, 2
Saturday, 7
scarf, 12

schedule, 16
script, 16
seat, 18
September, 15
serve, 16
shape, 9
shirt, 4
shoe, 2
shop, 6
shopper, 6
shopping mall, 17
shopping, F1-4
shorts, 12
shoulder, 12
show, 3
singer, 9
sink, 14
sir, 3
sister, 1
situation, 18
ski, 5
ski runs, 9
skier, 9
skin, 12
skirt, 4
sky-diving, F10-13
snow, 7
snowboarding, 9
soft drink, 6
someone, 9
something, 10
somewhere, 17
song, 7
sound, 9
spaghetti, 2
sports, 1
sports club, 5
sports shoes, 6
spring, 17
state, 3
statement, 10
stereo, 8
stereo equipment, 6
steps, F14-18
stocking, 4
store, F1-4
strangers, F14-18
street, 3
street address, 3
stress, 16
student, 1
stuff, 10
suburb, 3
subway station, 11
suit, 4
suitcase, 8
summer, 4
Sunday, 7
sunglasses, 4
supermarket, 2
surfing, 5
sushi, F10-13
sweater, 4
table, 10
tea, 18
teacher, 1
team, 9
telephone, 3
telephone numbers, 16
television, F10-13
tempura, 2
tennis, 5
test, 10
thing, 1
Thursday, F10-13
ticket, 13
tie, 4
time, 5
tiramisu, 2

tires, 18
title, 3
topic, 18
tour guide, F14-18
tourist, F14-18
town, 8
train, 11
train station, 11
transportation, 15
travel, 5
trends, 4
trip, 13
trouble, F5-9
TV, 5
type, 11
umbrella, 12
uncle, 10
university, 9
vacation, 17
Valentine's Day, 6
vest, 4
video, 7
vodka, 2
voice, 9
volleyball, 5
waiter, F1-4
waitress, F14-18
wall, F5-9
wallet, 14
water polo, 2
water sport, 2
way, 3
weather, 15
web, 5
wedding, 14
Wednesday, F10-13
week, 5
weekend, 7
weigh, 18
wife, 10
wig, 12
windows, 8
wine, 18
winter, 7
wire, 14,
woman, 12
world, 15
wrist, 4
year, 5
zip code, 3
zipper, 14